P9-DZN-095

COOKING *with* BEER

Publications International, Ltd.

Pictured on the front cover: Chicken Wings in Cerveza *(page 14)*.

Pictured on the back cover *(top to bottom)*: Coconut Shrimp *(page 22)*, Best Beef Brisket Sandwich Ever *(page 40)* and Beer-Braised Chili *(page 30)*.

ISBN-13: 978-1-4127-8181-7
ISBN-10: 1-4127-8181-7

Library of Congress Control Number: 2008940484

Manufactured in China.

8 7 6 5 4 3 2 1

Preparation/Cooking Times: Preparation times are based on the approximate amount of time required to assemble the recipe before cooking, baking, chilling or serving. These times include preparation steps such as measuring, chopping and mixing. The fact that some preparations and cooking can be done simultaneously is taken into account. Preparation of optional ingredients and serving suggestions is not included.

Contents

Beer Bites

Beer-Battered Mushrooms

1 cup all-purpose flour
½ teaspoon baking powder
½ teaspoon chili powder
¼ teaspoon salt, plus extra for seasoning
⅛ teaspoon black pepper
1 cup beer
1 egg, separated
1 pound small mushrooms
1½ quarts vegetable oil

1. Mix flour, baking powder, chili powder, salt and black pepper in medium bowl. Whisk together beer and egg yolk in small bowl. Wipe mushrooms clean with damp cloth or paper towel.

2. Beat egg white in medium bowl with electric mixer at medium speed until soft peaks form. Heat oil in 4-quart saucepan to 365°F.

3. Stir beer mixture into flour mixture just until blended. Fold in egg white.

4. Dip mushrooms into batter in batches and lower carefully into hot oil. Fry, turning with tongs or slotted spoon, until golden brown. Stir batter and allow oil to return to temperature between batches. Drain mushrooms on paper towels. Season with salt. Serve hot. *Makes 6 to 8 servings*

Mini Beer, Beef & Potato Turnovers

- 2 tablespoons olive oil
- 1½ cups chopped onions
- 2 cups chopped mushrooms
- ½ teaspoon salt
- ½ teaspoon dried thyme
- ⅛ teaspoon black pepper
- 1½ cups chopped cooked steak
- 1½ cups diced cooked potatoes
- 2 teaspoons Worcestershire sauce
- 1 cup dark beer
- All-purpose flour
- 2 packages refrigerated pie crusts (4 crusts)
- 1 egg
- 1 teaspoon water
- Beer Tarragon Mustard (recipe follows)

1. Preheat oven to 350°F. Spray 2 cookie sheets with nonstick cooking spray.

2. Heat oil in large skillet over medium heat. Add onions; cook and stir until softened. Add mushrooms; cook and stir 5 to 6 minutes. Sprinkle with salt, thyme and pepper. Stir in steak, potatoes and Worcestershire sauce. Pour in beer. Increase heat to high; cook and stir 5 minutes or until liquid is absorbed.

3. Unroll pie crusts on floured cutting board. Cut out circles using 4½-inch cutter. Reroll scraps and cut out additional circles. Place on prepared cookie sheets.

4. Place 2 tablespoons meat mixture in center of each circle and fold over; seal with fork. Poke with fork to vent. Whisk egg and water in small bowl and brush over turnovers. Bake 25 to 30 minutes or until golden brown. Serve with Beer Tarragon Mustard.

Makes 18 to 22 turnovers

Beer Tarragon Mustard

- ⅓ cup course grain mustard
- 2 tablespoons deli-style brown mustard
- 1 tablespoon chopped fresh tarragon
- 1 tablespoon beer
- 1 tablespoon honey

Combine all ingredients in small bowl. Cover and refrigerate until ready to serve.

Makes ½ cup mustard

Soft Beer Pretzels

3¼ cups all-purpose flour
1 package rapid-rise active dry yeast
1 teaspoon salt
⅔ cup beer
6½ cups water, divided
2 tablespoons vegetable oil
2 tablespoons baking soda
1 egg, beaten
Kosher salt

1. Combine 3 cups flour, yeast and salt in large bowl. Heat beer, ½ cup water and oil in small saucepan until hot. Add to flour mixture; beat with electric mixer at low speed until moistened. Beat in remaining flour, 1 tablespoon at a time, until soft dough forms. Turn dough onto lightly floured surface; knead for 5 to 6 minutes or until smooth and elastic. Cover; let rise in warm place 15 minutes.

2. Divide dough in half, then cut each half into 6 pieces. With lightly floured hands, roll each piece into 14-inch rope. (Cover remaining dough while working to prevent it from drying out.) Twist each rope into pretzel shape, pressing edges to seal. Place on greased baking sheets. Cover; let rise in warm place 15 minutes.

3. Preheat oven to 400°F. Bring 6 cups water to a boil in large saucepan; stir in baking soda. Working in batches, gently lower pretzels into boiling water; cook for 30 seconds, turning once. Using a slotted spoon, remove pretzels to wire rack coated with nonstick cooking spray.

4. Brush pretzels with egg and sprinkle with salt. Bake on ungreased baking sheet 10 minutes or until golden brown. Cool on wire rack.   *Makes 1 dozen pretzels*

Potted Beer and Cheddar

8 ounces cream cheese, softened
4 tablespoons CABOT® Unsalted Butter, softened
4 cups grated CABOT® Sharp Cheddar (about 1 pound)
1 tablespoon minced fresh chives
1 tablespoon chopped fresh parsley
1 teaspoon Worcestershire sauce
1 teaspoon Dijon mustard
1 teaspoon prepared horseradish
½ clove garlic, minced
¼ teaspoon ground black pepper
2 to 3 drops hot pepper sauce
¼ to ½ cup flat beer

1. With electric mixer, beat together cream cheese and butter until well blended. Mix in cheese.

2. Mix in all remaining ingredients except beer. Add enough beer to make spread of desired consistency. (Mixture will thicken further after chilling.)

3. Pack into earthenware crock or other ceramic dish; cover and refrigerate for several hours to allow flavors to blend. Serve with apple slices and dark rye bread or crackers.

Makes about 3 cups

Note: Spread can be made several weeks in advance.

Favorite recipe from **Marcy Goldman**

Tipsy Chicken Wraps

1 tablespoon dark sesame oil
1 pound ground chicken
8 ounces firm tofu, diced
½ red bell pepper, diced
3 green onions, sliced
1 tablespoon minced fresh ginger
2 cloves garlic, minced
½ cup Asian beer
⅓ cup hoisin sauce
1 teaspoon hot chili paste
½ cup chopped peanuts
2 heads Boston lettuce, separated into large leaves
Whole fresh chives (optional)

1. Heat oil in large skillet over medium heat. Brown chicken 4 to 6 minutes, stirring to break up meat. Drain fat. Add tofu, bell pepper, green onions, ginger and garlic. Cook and stir until onions are softened. Add beer, hoisin sauce and chili paste. Cook until heated through. Stir in peanuts.

2. Place spoonful of chicken mixture in center of each lettuce leaf. Roll up to enclose filling. Tie chives around filled leaves to secure, if desired. *Makes about 20 wraps*

Beer-Braised Meatballs

1 pound ground beef
$\frac{1}{2}$ cup Italian bread crumbs
$\frac{1}{2}$ cup grated Parmesan cheese
2 eggs, lightly beaten
$\frac{1}{3}$ cup finely chopped onion
2 cloves garlic, minced
$\frac{1}{2}$ teaspoon black pepper
$\frac{1}{4}$ teaspoon salt
1 bottle (12 ounces) light-colored beer
$1\frac{1}{2}$ cups tomato sauce
1 cup ketchup
2 tablespoons tomato paste
$\frac{1}{2}$ cup packed brown sugar

1. Preheat oven to 400°F. Line broiler pan with foil; spray rack with nonstick cooking spray. Combine beef, bread crumbs, cheese, eggs, onion, garlic, pepper and salt in large bowl; shape mixture into 1-inch balls.

2. Place meatballs on broiling rack. Bake 10 minutes or until browned.

3. Combine beer, tomato sauce, ketchup, tomato paste and sugar in large Dutch oven; bring to a boil. Add meatballs and reduce heat. Cover and simmer 20 to 30 minutes or until meatballs are cooked through, stirring occasionally.   *Makes 20 meatballs*

Chicken Wings in Cerveza

1½ pounds chicken wings or drummettes
   1 teaspoon salt
   1 teaspoon dried thyme
   ⅛ teaspoon black pepper
   1 bottle (12 ounces) Mexican beer

1. Cut off and discard wing tips. Cut each wing in half at joint. Place chicken in shallow bowl; sprinkle with salt, thyme and pepper. Pour beer over chicken; toss to coat. Cover and refrigerate 2 hours or up to 6 hours.

2. Preheat oven to 375°F. Line shallow baking pan with foil; spray with nonstick cooking spray.

3. Drain chicken, reserving marinade. Arrange chicken on prepared pan in single layer. Bake 40 minutes or until chicken is well browned on all sides, turning and basting with reserved marinade occasionally. (Do not brush with marinade during last 5 minutes of baking.) Discard remaining marinade. Serve warm or at room temperature.

Makes 6 servings

TIP: Most Mexican beers are light in color and body and are lagers similar to popular beers sold in the U.S. Choose your favorite for this recipe. Food safety is a serious concern with any marinade that comes into contact with raw meat. In this case, since the marinade is used for basting, it's important to stop brushing it on at least five minutes before the end of baking time. This insures that any harmful bacteria present in the marinade have been destroyed by the heat of the oven.

Vegetable Cheese Roll-Ups

2 tablespoons butter
½ cup diced onion
½ cup diced red bell pepper
½ cup finely diced mushrooms
½ cup broccoli florets
½ cup beer
¼ teaspoon salt
¼ teaspoon black pepper
1 package refrigerated crescent roll dough
½ cup (2 ounces) shredded Cheddar cheese

1. Melt butter in medium skillet over medium heat. Add onion and bell pepper; cook and stir about 3 minutes or until tender. Add mushrooms, broccoli, beer, salt and black pepper. Cook 5 minutes or until beer has evaporated; let cool.

2. Preheat oven to 375°F. Separate crescent roll dough into 8 pieces. Sprinkle about 1 tablespoon cheese on wide end of 1 dough piece. Top with 1 tablespoon filling. Roll dough over filling; seal closed and bend into crescent shape. Place on ungreased baking sheet. Repeat with remaining pieces of dough.

3. Bake 11 to 13 minutes or until rolls are golden brown. Serve warm.

Makes 8 servings

TIP: Cultivated white mushrooms are usually called button mushrooms. Brown mushrooms are often labeled "baby bellas" or "cremini mushrooms". They generally have a slightly richer flavor and denser texture than the white variety. Portobello mushrooms are fully matured forms of cremini mushrooms. Brown and white cultivated mushrooms are interchangeable in recipes.

Stout Beef Bundles

1 pound ground beef
½ cup sliced green onions
1 medium clove garlic, minced
⅔ cup chopped water chestnuts
½ cup chopped red bell pepper
¼ cup stout
2 tablespoons hoisin sauce
1 tablespoon soy sauce
2 tablespoons chopped fresh cilantro
1 or 2 heads leaf lettuce, separated into leaves

1. Brown beef 6 to 8 minutes in large skillet over medium-high heat, stirring to break up meat. Drain fat. Add green onions and garlic; cook and stir until tender. Stir in water chestnuts, bell pepper, stout, hoisin and soy sauce. Cook, stirring occasionally, until bell pepper is crisp-tender and most of liquid has evaporated.

2. Stir in cilantro. Spoon beef mixture evenly onto individual lettuce leaves; sprinkle with additional hoisin sauce, if desired. Wrap lettuce leaves around beef mixture to make bundles. *Makes 8 servings*

Little Ribs in Paprika Sauce

1 slab (about 1½ pounds) baby back pork ribs, split horizontally
1 can (about 14 ounces) chicken broth
1 cup beer
1 tablespoon olive oil
2 teaspoons dried oregano
2 teaspoons paprika or smoked paprika
4 cloves garlic, minced
½ teaspoon salt
¼ teaspoon black pepper

1. Cut ribs into individual pieces. Place ribs, broth, beer, oil, oregano, paprika, garlic, salt and pepper in large saucepan. Bring to a boil over medium-high heat. Reduce heat. Simmer, covered, 1 hour or until meat is tender and begins to separate from bones.

2. Remove ribs to serving plate; keep warm. Skim and discard fat from cooking liquid. Bring to a boil over medium heat. Reduce heat; simmer until sauce is reduced to about 3 tablespoons. Spoon sauce over ribs. Serve immediately. *Makes 6 to 8 servings*

TIP: Get your butcher to cut the slab of ribs horizontally to make shorter pieces for this appetizer so they're easier to handle. Use baby back ribs (also called loin back ribs) which are smaller and less fatty than regular spareribs.

Thick Potato Chips with Beer Ketchup

3 baking potatoes, scrubbed
I quart peanut oil
  Sea salt and black pepper
  Beer Ketchup (recipe follows)

I. Heat oil in deep pan (oil should come up sides at least 3 inches) to 345°F.

2. Slice potatoes into ¼-inch-thick slices and place in oil in batches. Fry 2 to 3 minutes per side, flipping to brown evenly. Drain on paper towels and immediately season with salt and pepper.

3. Serve with Beer Ketchup.

Makes 4 servings

Tip: If the potatoes begin browning too quickly, turn down the heat and wait for the oil to cool to the proper temperature. Too high a temperature will burn the outside but not cook the potatoes completely. Too low a temperature will make the chips soggy.

Beer Ketchup

¾ cup ketchup
¼ cup beer
 I tablespoon Worcestershire sauce
¼ teaspoon onion powder
⅛ teaspoon ground red pepper

Mix all ingredients in small saucepan. Bring to a boil. Reduce heat; simmer 2 to 3 minutes. Let cool. Cover and store in refrigerator until ready to use.

Makes about ¾ cup ketchup

Coconut Shrimp

Vegetable oil for frying
1¼ cups beer
¾ cup all-purpose flour
½ cup CREAM OF WHEAT® Hot Cereal (Instant, 1-minute, 2½-minute or
    10-minute cook time), uncooked
2 teaspoons salt
2 teaspoons ground paprika
2 cups unsweetened shredded coconut, divided
1 pound uncooked shrimp, cleaned, peeled, deveined
    Asian duck sauce or other dipping sauce (optional)

1. Preheat oil in deep fryer or heavy saucepan to 360°F. Combine beer, flour, Cream of Wheat, salt and paprika in medium bowl. Stir in 1 cup coconut; mix well. Let stand 5 minutes. Place remaining 1 cup coconut in shallow bowl.

2. Place shrimp into batter; stir to coat. Remove shrimp individually; dip each shrimp into coconut, covering evenly. Fry shrimp in batches 4 minutes or until golden brown. (Cook larger shrimp 1 to 2 minutes longer if necessary.) Remove with slotted spoon and drain on paper towels. Serve immediately with dipping sauce, if desired. *Makes 4 servings*

Tip: Serve these delicious shrimp with a crispy Asian-style salad for a tasty meal. They also make great individual appetizers.

Prep Time: 10 minutes • **Start to Finish Time:** 20 minutes

Spiced Beer Fondue

1 bottle (12 ounces) ale or lager
2 cups (8 ounces) shredded Gruyère cheese
1 cup (4 ounces) shredded Cheddar cheese
2 tablespoons all-purpose flour
1 teaspoon coarse grain mustard
$\frac{1}{4}$ teaspoon salt
$\frac{1}{8}$ teaspoon ground red pepper
$\frac{1}{4}$ teaspoon ground nutmeg
   Bread cubes, cooked potato pieces, apple slices and/or chopped vegetables

1. Bring ale to a boil in medium saucepan; simmer over medium heat until it stops foaming, about 5 minutes. Reduce heat to low.

2. Toss cheeses with flour in medium bowl. Gradually add cheese mixture to ale while stirring constantly. Add mustard, salt and ground red pepper. Cook gently, stirring constantly, until cheese is melted. Transfer to fondue pot over low heat and sprinkle with nutmeg. Serve with bread cubes, cooked potato pieces, apple slices and/or your favorite chopped vegetables. *Makes 4 servings*

Tip: Stirring constantly while cooking the fondue is essential. If left still over heat, the cheese can easily burn.

Beef & Brew

Beef Pot Pie

½ cup all-purpose flour
1 teaspoon salt, divided
½ teaspoon black pepper, divided
1½ pounds lean beef stew meat
2 tablespoons olive oil
1 pound new red potatoes, cubed
2 cups baby carrots
1 cup frozen pearl onions, thawed
1 parsnip, peeled and cut into 1-inch pieces
1 cup stout
¾ cup beef broth
1 teaspoon chopped fresh thyme *or* ½ teaspoon dried thyme
1 prepared 9-inch pie crust, at room temperature

1. Preheat oven to 350°F. Combine flour, ½ teaspoon salt and ¼ teaspoon pepper in large resealable food storage bag. Add beef. Seal bag; shake to coat.

2. Heat oil in large skillet over medium-high heat. Add beef in batches; brown on all sides. Transfer beef to large casserole. Add potatoes, carrots, onions and parsnip to casserole; mix well.

3. Add stout, broth, thyme, remaining ½ teaspoon salt and ¼ teaspoon pepper to same skillet. Bring to a boil, scraping browned bits from bottom of pan. Pour into casserole.

4. Cover; bake 2½ to 3 hours or until meat is fork-tender, stirring once. Remove cover; let stand at room temperature 15 minutes.

5. *Increase oven temperature to 425°F.* Place pie crust over casserole and press edges to seal. Cut slits in crust to vent. Bake 15 to 20 minutes or until crust is golden brown. Cool slightly before serving. *Makes 4 to 6 servings*

Oxtail Soup with Beer

2½ pounds oxtails (beef or veal)
1 large onion, sliced
4 carrots, cut into 1-inch chunks, divided
3 stalks celery, cut into 1-inch chunks, divided
2 sprigs fresh parsley
5 peppercorns
1 bay leaf
4 cups beef broth
1 cup dark beer
2 cups diced baking potatoes
1 teaspoon salt
2 tablespoons chopped fresh parsley (optional)

1. Combine oxtails, onion, 2 carrots, 1 stalk celery, parsley sprigs, peppercorns and bay leaf in large saucepan. Pour broth and beer over mixture; bring to a boil. Reduce heat; simmer, covered, 3 hours or until meat is falling off bones.

2. Remove oxtails and set aside. Strain broth and return to pan; skim off excess fat. Add remaining 2 carrots, 2 stalks celery and potatoes; bring to a simmer over medium heat. Cook 10 to 15 minutes or until vegetables are tender.

3. Remove meat from oxtails and return meat to pan. Stir in salt and heat through. Ladle soup into bowls and sprinkle with chopped parsley, if desired. *Makes 4 servings*

TIP: Oxtails were once really from oxen (castrated bulls), but the term now refers to the tail of a beef animal. Oxtails are ideal for soup. They are bony, tough and full of connective tissue, but long, slow cooking releases the flavor and gelatin and gives a satisfying, meaty body to the dish.

Beer-Braised Chili

2 tablespoons vegetable oil

2 pounds boneless beef chuck roast or stew meat, cut into ¾-inch cubes

1 large onion, chopped

4 cloves garlic, minced

1 tablespoon chili powder

1 tablespoon ground cumin

1¼ teaspoons salt

1 teaspoon dried oregano

½ teaspoon ground red pepper

1 can (about 14 ounces) Mexican-style stewed tomatoes, undrained

1 bottle or can (12 ounces) light-colored beer

½ cup salsa

1 can (about 15 ounces) black beans, rinsed and drained

1 can (about 15 ounces) red beans or pinto beans, rinsed and drained

Toppings (optional): chopped cilantro, thinly sliced green onions, shredded Chihuahua or Cheddar cheese, sliced pickled jalapeño peppers and sour cream

1. Heat oil in large saucepan or Dutch oven over medium-high heat. Add beef, onion and garlic; cook and stir 5 minutes. Sprinkle chili powder, cumin, salt, oregano and red pepper over mixture; mix well. Add tomatoes, beer and salsa; bring to a boil. Reduce heat; cover and simmer 1¼ hours or until beef is very tender, stirring occasionally.

2. Stir in beans. Simmer, uncovered, 20 minutes or until thickened. Serve chili with desired toppings.

Makes about 8 cups chili

TIP: To take this chili to a tailgating party, cover the hot chili securely and wrap the container well in newspaper or towels. It will stay warm up to 1½ hours. Wrap the toppings separately in small containers. If you transport the chili chilled, reheat it in a covered pot on a grill 15 to 20 minutes or until heated through.

Smoky Barbecued Beef Sandwiches

2 large onions, cut into thin slices
1 beef brisket (about 3 pounds), trimmed
½ teaspoon salt
¾ cup light-colored beer
½ cup packed light brown sugar
½ cup ketchup
1 tablespoon plus 1½ teaspoons Worcestershire sauce
1 tablespoon plus 1½ teaspoons soy sauce
2 cloves garlic, minced
2 canned chipotle peppers in adobo sauce, minced, plus 1 teaspoon sauce*
6 hoagie or kaiser rolls, split and toasted

*For spicier flavor, add 1 to 2 additional teaspoons sauce.

1. Preheat oven to 325°F. Separate onion slices into rings. Place in bottom of large roasting pan.

2. Place brisket, fat side up, over onions; sprinkle with salt. Combine beer, brown sugar, ketchup, Worcestershire sauce, soy sauce, garlic and chipotle peppers with sauce in small bowl; pour over brisket.

3. Cover with heavy-duty foil or lid. Roast 3 to 3½ hours or until brisket is fork-tender.

4. Transfer brisket to cutting board; tent with foil. Let stand 10 minutes. (Brisket and sauce may be prepared ahead up to this point. Cool and cover separately. Refrigerate up to 1 day before reheating and serving.)

5. Transfer juices to large saucepan; skim fat. Cook over medium heat until thickened, stirring frequently.

6. Carve brisket across grain into thin slices. Transfer slices to sauce; heat through. Serve slices and sauce in rolls.

Makes 6 servings

Hearty Beefy Beer Soup

1 tablespoon vegetable oil
¾ pound round steak, cut into ½-inch cubes
1 large onion, chopped
2 medium carrots, sliced
2 stalks celery, diced
5 cups beef broth
1 bottle (12 ounces) stout or dark ale
¾ teaspoon dried oregano
¼ teaspoon salt
⅛ teaspoon black pepper
1 small zucchini, cut into ½-inch cubes
4 ounces mushrooms, sliced
1 can (about 15 ounces) kidney beans, rinsed and drained

1. Heat oil in 5-quart Dutch oven over medium heat. Add beef, onion, carrots and celery. Cook and stir until meat is browned and carrots and celery are beginning to soften.

2. Stir in broth, stout, oregano, salt and pepper. Bring to a boil over high heat. Reduce heat to medium-low; simmer, uncovered, 45 minutes or until beef is fork-tender.

3. Stir zucchini, mushrooms and beans into soup. Bring to a boil over high heat. Reduce heat to medium-low; simmer, uncovered, 5 minutes or until zucchini is tender. Ladle into bowls. *Makes 6 servings*

Beef Cabbage Rolls with Beer

12 ounces lean ground beef
12 ounces lean ground pork
 1 medium onion, chopped
 1 can (15 ounces) tomato sauce, divided
 1 teaspoon salt
 1 teaspoon dried thyme
¼ teaspoon black pepper
 1 large green cabbage
 1 bottle (12 ounces) beer
   Salt and black pepper
   Chopped fresh parsley (optional)

SLOW COOKER DIRECTIONS

1. Combine beef, pork, onion, 1 cup tomato sauce, salt, thyme and pepper in large bowl; mix well.

2. Pour ¼ cup tomato sauce into 5-quart slow cooker.

3. Cut out core from cabbage and carefully remove leaves. Place a golf ball-sized mound of meat mixture in center of large cabbage leaf, edges curling upward. Starting with the thickest side, fold leaf over meat mixture, burrito-style. Place fold side down into slow cooker. Repeat with remaining meat and cabbage leaves, stacking as necessary.

4. Pour beer over cabbage rolls. Pour remaining tomato sauce on top of rolls.

5. Cover; cook on LOW 5 hours. Halfway through cooking time, push cabbage rolls under liquid to submerge them. Season to taste with salt and pepper before serving. Sprinkle with chopped parsley, if desired. *Makes about 12 rolls*

TIP: For a thicker sauce, mix 2 tablespoons cornstarch with ¼ cup water in small bowl until smooth. Stir into liquid in slow cooker. Cook, uncovered, on HIGH until thickened.

Slow Cooker Beer Bolognese

3 slices bacon, chopped
1 large onion, chopped
1 carrot, chopped
1 celery stalk, chopped
2 cloves garlic, minced
3 teaspoons olive oil, divided
½ pound mushrooms, sliced
¾ pound lean ground beef
¾ pound lean ground pork
1 can (28 ounces) tomato purée
1 bottle (12 ounces) dark beer
1 cup beef broth
1 tablespoon tomato paste
1 teaspoon salt
¼ teaspoon black pepper
¼ teaspoon red pepper flakes
   Hot cooked pasta
   Shaved Parmesan cheese and chopped fresh parsley (optional)

SLOW COOKER DIRECTIONS

1. Cook bacon in large skillet over medium-high heat. Remove and drain on paper towels.

2. Add onion, carrot and celery to same skillet; cook and stir until beginning to brown, about 5 minutes. Add garlic; cook and stir 1 to 2 minutes. Transfer vegetables to slow cooker. Add 1 teaspoon oil to skillet. Add mushrooms; cook and stir until beginning to brown. Add to slow cooker.

3. Heat remaining 2 teaspoons oil in skillet. Brown beef and pork over medium-high heat, stirring to break up meat. Drain fat. Transfer meat to slow cooker. Stir in bacon, tomato purée, beer, broth, tomato paste, salt, black pepper and red pepper flakes. Cover; cook on LOW 8 to 10 hours. Serve over pasta. Top with Parmesan and parsley, if desired. *Makes 8 servings*

Deviled Beef Short Rib Stew

4 pounds beef short ribs, trimmed
2 pounds small red potatoes, scrubbed and scored
8 carrots, peeled and cut into chunks
2 onions, cut into thick wedges
1 bottle (12 ounces) beer or non-alcoholic malt beverage
8 tablespoons *French's*® Spicy Brown Mustard, divided
3 tablespoons *French's*® Worcestershire Sauce, divided
2 tablespoons cornstarch

SLOW COOKER DIRECTIONS

1. Broil ribs 6 inches from heat on rack in broiler pan 10 minutes or until well browned, turning once. Place vegetables in bottom of slow cooker. Place ribs on top of vegetables.

2. Combine beer, *6 tablespoons* mustard and *2 tablespoons* Worcestershire in medium bowl. Pour into slow cooker. Cover and cook on HIGH setting for 5 hours* or until meat is tender.

3. Transfer meat and vegetables to platter; keep warm. Strain fat from broth; pour broth into saucepan. Combine cornstarch with *2 tablespoons cold water* in small bowl. Stir into broth with remaining *2 tablespoons* mustard and *1 tablespoon* Worcestershire. Heat to boiling. Reduce heat to medium-low. Cook 1 to 2 minutes or until thickened, stirring often. Pass gravy with meat and vegetables. Serve meat with additional mustard.

Makes 6 servings (with 3 cups gravy)

*Or cook 10 hours on LOW setting.

Hint: Prepare ingredients the night before for quick assembly in the morning. Keep refrigerated until ready to use.

Tip: Use a barley wine or spiced winter ale in this stew for an even bolder beef flavor.

Best Beef Brisket Sandwich Ever

 1 beef brisket (about 3 pounds)
 2 cups apple cider, divided
⅓ cup chopped fresh thyme *or* 2 tablespoons dried thyme
 1 head garlic, cloves separated, crushed and peeled
 2 tablespoons whole black peppercorns
 1 tablespoon mustard seeds
 1 tablespoon Cajun seasoning
 1 teaspoon ground cumin
 1 teaspoon celery seeds
 1 teaspoon ground allspice
 2 to 4 whole cloves
 1 bottle (12 ounces) dark beer
10 to 12 sourdough sandwich rolls, halved

SLOW COOKER DIRECTIONS

1. Place brisket, ½ cup cider, thyme, garlic, peppercorns, mustard seeds, Cajun seasoning, cumin, celery seeds, allspice and cloves in large resealable food storage bag. Seal bag; marinate in refrigerator overnight.

2. Place brisket and marinade in slow cooker. Add remaining 1½ cups apple cider and beer. Cover; cook on LOW 10 hours or until brisket is fork-tender.

3. Slice brisket and place on sandwich rolls. Strain sauce; drizzle over meat.

Makes 10 to 12 servings

TIP: Beer makes an excellent ingredient for a marinade. The enzymes in beer, which is a fermented brew, can help tenderize tough cuts of meat. When choosing which beer to use in cooking, always choose one that you enjoy drinking.

Savory Braised Beef

4 slices bacon
2 pounds boneless beef chuck or round steak, cut into 1-inch cubes
1 large clove garlic, finely chopped
1 envelope LIPTON® RECIPE SECRETS® Onion Soup Mix*
1 can or bottle (12 ounces) beer or 1½ cups water
1 cup water
1 tablespoon red wine vinegar
  Hot cooked rice

*Also terrific with LIPTON® RECIPE SECRETS® Onion Mushroom or Beefy Onion Soup Mix.

1. In Dutch oven or 6-quart saucepan, brown bacon until crisp. Remove bacon, crumble and set aside; reserve 1 tablespoon drippings.

2. Brown beef in two batches in reserved drippings. Remove beef and set aside.

3. Add garlic to drippings and cook over medium heat, stirring frequently, 30 seconds. Return beef to Dutch oven. Add soup mix blended with beer and 1 cup water. Bring to a boil over high heat.

4. Reduce heat to low and simmer, covered, stirring occasionally, 1 hour 15 minutes or until beef is tender. Skim fat, if necessary. Stir in vinegar and sprinkle with bacon. Serve over rice. *Makes 4 servings*

Western Barbecue Burgers with Beer Barbecue Sauce

8 slices thick-sliced bacon
1 cup smokehouse-style barbecue sauce
$\frac{1}{4}$ cup brown ale
$\frac{1}{2}$ teaspoon salt
$\frac{1}{4}$ teaspoon black pepper
1$\frac{1}{2}$ pounds lean ground beef
    Nonstick cooking spray
1 red onion, sliced into $\frac{1}{2}$-inch-thick rounds
4 hamburger buns
    Lettuce leaves
    Sliced tomatoes

1. Cook bacon in skillet over medium-high heat. Drain on paper towels; set aside. Pour barbecue sauce, ale, salt and pepper into small saucepan. Bring mixture to a boil; boil 1 minute. Set aside.

2. Shape beef into 4 patties. Season with salt and pepper, if desired.

3. Spray grill pan or large skillet with nonstick cooking spray. Heat over medium-high heat. Add onion slices and cook, turning often, until softened and slightly charred, about 4 minutes. Remove and set aside. Add beef patties to grill pan. Cook 3 to 5 minutes per side or until 160°F.

4. Serve patties on buns with onions, bacon, barbecue sauce, lettuce and tomatoes.

Makes 4 burgers

Beef Stew

2 tablespoons olive or vegetable oil
3 pounds beef chuck, trimmed and cut into 2-inch chunks
2 teaspoons salt
$\frac{1}{2}$ teaspoon black pepper
3 medium onions, halved and sliced
6 medium carrots, cut into $\frac{1}{2}$-inch pieces
$\frac{1}{2}$ pound sliced mushrooms
$\frac{1}{4}$ pound smoked ham, cut into $\frac{1}{4}$-inch pieces
2 tablespoons minced garlic
1 can (about 15 ounces) stout
1 can (about 14 ounces) beef broth
1 teaspoon sugar
1 teaspoon herbes de Provence or dried thyme
1 teaspoon Worcestershire sauce
2 tablespoons cornstarch
$\frac{1}{3}$ cup cold water
3 tablespoons chopped fresh parsley
Hot cooked wide noodles

1. Heat oil in large Dutch oven over medium-high heat. Add half of beef; sprinkle with salt and pepper. Brown beef on all sides, about 8 minutes. Remove to bowl and repeat with remaining beef.

2. Lower heat to medium. Add onions to Dutch oven; cook 10 minutes, stirring often. Stir in carrots, mushrooms, ham and garlic. Cook and stir 10 minutes or until onions are softened, scraping any brown bits from bottom of Dutch oven.

3. Return beef to Dutch oven. Pour in stout and broth. (Liquid should just cover beef and vegetables; add water if needed.) Add sugar, herbes de Provence and Worcestershire sauce; stir to combine. Bring to a boil. Reduce heat to low. Cover; simmer 2 hours or until meat is fork-tender.

4. Skim off fat. Stir cornstarch into $\frac{1}{3}$ cup cold water in small bowl. Stir into stew; simmer 5 minutes. Stir in parsley. Serve stew over noodles. *Makes 8 servings*

Beer-Braised Brisket

3 slices thick-cut bacon, diced
1 flat-cut beef brisket (about 3 pounds)
2 large onions, cut into thin slices
1 bottle (12 ounces) dark beer
3 cups beef broth
2 tablespoons chopped fresh parsley

1. Preheat oven to 325°F. Cook bacon in Dutch oven over medium heat until crisp. Remove bacon to paper towels. Brown brisket on both sides in Dutch oven. Remove to platter.

2. Pour off all but 2 tablespoons fat. Add onions; cook and stir over medium-high heat 3 to 4 minutes or until softened.

3. Add beer to Dutch oven. Bring to a boil over medium-high heat, stirring frequently and scraping up any browned bits from bottom of pan. Add brisket and broth; bring to a boil. Cover; transfer to oven. Bake 3½ to 4 hours or until fork-tender.

4. Remove brisket to cutting board; let rest 10 minutes. Using slotted spoon, remove onions and set aside. Boil remaining liquid over high heat until slightly thickened.

5. Slice brisket. Top with onions, sauce, bacon and parsley. *Makes 4 to 6 servings*

Beef & Brew   47

Game Plan

Pulled Pork Sandwiches

2 tablespoons kosher salt
2 tablespoons packed light brown sugar
2 tablespoons paprika
1 teaspoon dry mustard
1 teaspoon black pepper
1 boneless pork shoulder roast (about 3 pounds)
1½ cups stout
½ cup cider vinegar
6 to 8 large hamburger buns, split
¾ cup barbecue sauce

1. Preheat oven to 325°F. Combine salt, sugar, paprika, dry mustard and pepper in small bowl; mix well. Rub into pork.

2. Place pork in 4-quart Dutch oven. Add stout and vinegar. Cover; bake 3 hours or until meat is fork-tender. Cool 15 to 30 minutes or until cool enough to handle.

3. Shred pork into large pieces. Serve warm on buns with barbecue sauce.

Makes 6 to 8 servings

TIP: Beer can be divided into two main categories, ale and lager, based on the type of fermentation. Ales are top-fermented and tend to be heartier and more complex than lagers. Irish stout is probably the best known ale. The term stout comes from an archaic word meaning strong, and for many years stout was considered a healthy drink and a pick-me-up. In the 1900s, it was even prescribed as a tonic for nursing mothers.

Beer and Chipotle Fish Tacos

1 1/2 pounds cod, grouper or other white fish fillets, cut into thin strips
1 bottle (12 ounces) pale ale
1/2 cup yellow cornmeal
1 teaspoon chipotle chili powder, or more to taste
1/2 teaspoon salt
2 tablespoons olive oil
8 (6-inch) white corn tortillas, warmed
Shredded cabbage
Chopped tomatoes
Toppings (optional): chopped fresh cilantro, salsa, sour cream and lime wedges

1. Place fish in shallow dish. Pour beer over fish; marinate 15 to 30 minutes.

2. Combine cornmeal, chipotle chili powder and salt in another shallow dish. Drain fish; coat in cornmeal mixture.

3. Heat oil in large skillet over medium-high heat. Cook fish 3 minutes on each side or until golden brown.

4. Serve fish in tortillas with cabbage, tomatoes and toppings, if desired.

Makes 8 tacos

Mustard Beer Biscuits

2 cups all-purpose flour
2 teaspoons baking powder
3/4 teaspoon salt
1/4 cup cold shortening
1/4 cup (1/2 stick) cold butter
1/2 cup beer
1 tablespoon plus 1 teaspoon prepared mustard, divided
1 tablespoon milk

1. Preheat oven to 425°F. Combine flour, baking powder and salt in large bowl. Cut in shortening and butter until mixture resembles coarse crumbs. Combine beer and 1 tablespoon mustard in small bowl; stir into flour mixture just until blended. Turn onto floured surface; knead gently 8 times.

2. Pat dough to 1/2-inch thickness. Cut out biscuits with 2-inch round biscuit cutter. Reroll scraps and cut out additional biscuits. Place 1-inch apart on greased baking sheet. Combine remaining 1 teaspoon mustard with milk in small bowl and brush over tops. Bake 13 to 15 minutes or until lightly browned. *Makes about 1 dozen biscuits*

Beer and Chipotle Fish Tacos

Cerveza Chicken Enchilada Casserole

    2 cups water
    1 bottle (12 ounces) Mexican beer, divided
    1 stalk celery, chopped
    1 small carrot, chopped
      Juice of 1 lime
    1 teaspoon salt
1½ pounds boneless skinless chicken breasts
    1 can (about 10 ounces) enchilada sauce
    1 bag (9 ounces) white corn tortilla chips
    ½ medium onion, chopped
    3 cups (12 ounces) shredded Cheddar cheese
      Sour cream, sliced olives and cilantro (optional)

SLOW COOKER DIRECTIONS

1. Place water, 1 cup beer, celery, carrot, lime juice and salt in large saucepan. Bring to a boil over high heat. Place chicken breasts in water mixture; reduce heat to a simmer. Cook 12 to 14 minutes or until chicken is no longer pink in center. Cool and shred into bite-sized pieces.

2. Spoon ½ cup enchilada sauce in 5-quart slow cooker. Arrange tortilla chips over sauce. Layer with one third of shredded chicken and one third of chopped onion. Sprinkle with 1 cup cheese. Pour ½ cup enchilada sauce over cheese. Repeat layers twice, pouring remaining beer over casserole before adding last cup of cheese.

3. Cover; cook on LOW 3½ to 4 hours. Garnish with sour cream, sliced olives and cilantro. *Makes 4 to 6 servings*

Cerveza Chicken Enchilada Casserole

Pastrami Sandwiches with Mustard

1½ cups low-sodium beef broth
1 cup dark beer
1 teaspoon Worcestershire sauce
1 pound thinly sliced pastrami
6 sandwich rolls
12 slices Swiss cheese
Dijon mustard

1. Heat broiler to 500°F. Combine broth, beer and Worcestershire sauce in small saucepan. Bring to a boil. Reduce heat to low. Separate layers of pastrami and add to pan. Cook until pastrami is heated through.

2. Split sandwich rolls and place on baking sheet. Arrange pastrami on bottom half of each roll. Reserve cooking liquid and keep warm. Top each roll with 2 slices cheese. Broil 1 to 2 minutes or until cheese is melted and bubbly. Serve with mustard and reserved cooking liquid for dipping. *Makes 6 servings*

Asparagus with Honey-Garlic Sauce

1 pound asparagus
¼ cup Dijon mustard
¼ cup dark ale or beer
3 tablespoons honey
½ teaspoon minced garlic
¼ teaspoon crushed dried thyme leaves
¼ teaspoon salt

Add asparagus to boiling, salted water; cook, covered, about 2 minutes or until barely tender. Drain. Combine mustard, ale, honey, garlic, thyme and salt; mix well. Pour over asparagus. *Makes 4 servings*

Favorite recipe from **National Honey Board**

Jambalaya

1 package (about 16 ounces) Cajun sausage, sliced
1 cup chopped onion
1 cup chopped green bell pepper
2 cloves garlic, minced
2 cups uncooked rice
2 cups low-sodium chicken broth
1 bottle (12 ounces) pale ale
1 can (about 14 ounces) diced tomatoes with green pepper, onion and celery
1 teaspoon Cajun seasoning
1 pound medium cooked shrimp, peeled and deveined
   Chopped fresh parsley (optional)
   Hot pepper sauce (optional)

1. Brown sausage in large Dutch oven over medium-high heat; drain. Add onion, bell pepper and garlic; cook and stir 2 to 3 minutes or until tender. Add rice, broth and pale ale. Bring to a boil. Cover; reduce heat to low. Simmer 20 minutes, stirring occasionally.

2. Stir in tomatoes and Cajun seasoning; cook 5 minutes. Add shrimp and cook 2 to 3 minutes or until heated through. Sprinkle with parsley and hot pepper sauce.

Makes 6 to 8 servings

TIP: Cajun cooking is a robust combination of French and southern cuisines with lots of spice. Andouille, the best known Cajun sausage, is used in dishes such as gumbo and jambalaya. It is a spicy smoked sausage made of pork.

Spicy Ale Shrimp

3 bottles (12 ounces each) beer, divided
1 tablespoon seafood boil seasoning blend
1 teaspoon mustard seeds
1 teaspoon red pepper flakes
1 lemon, sliced into quarters
1 pound large raw shrimp, peeled and deveined (with tails on)
  Dipping Sauce (recipe follows)

1. Fill large saucepan half full with water. Add 2 bottles of beer, seafood boil seasoning, mustard seeds and red pepper flakes. Squeeze lemon juice into saucepan and add lemon quarters. Bring mixture to a boil over medium-high heat.

2. Meanwhile, pour remaining 1 bottle of beer into large bowl half-filled with ice; set aside.

3. Add shrimp to saucepan. Cover; remove from heat. Let sit 3 minutes or until shrimp are pink and opaque. Drain; transfer shrimp to bowl of chilled beer and ice. When cool, remove shrimp from bowl; arrange on platter. Serve with Dipping Sauce.

Makes 15 to 20 shrimp

Dipping Sauce

1 cup ketchup
1 tablespoon prepared horseradish
1 to 2 teaspoons chili-garlic paste
  Juice of 1 lime

Combine ketchup, horseradish, chili-garlic paste and lime juice in small bowl. Cover; refrigerate 1 hour.

Makes about 1 cup sauce

Chicken Burgers with White Cheddar

1¼ pounds ground chicken
1 cup dry bread crumbs
½ cup diced red bell pepper
½ cup ground walnuts
¼ cup sliced green onions
¼ cup light-colored beer
2 tablespoons chopped fresh parsley
2 tablespoons lemon juice
2 cloves garlic, minced
¾ teaspoon salt
⅛ teaspoon black pepper
Nonstick cooking spray
4 slices white Cheddar cheese
4 whole wheat buns
Dijon mustard
Lettuce leaves

1. Combine chicken, bread crumbs, bell pepper, walnuts, green onions, beer, parsley, lemon juice, garlic, salt and black pepper in large bowl; mix lightly. Shape chicken mixture into 4 patties.

2. Spray large skillet with cooking spray; heat over medium-high heat. Cook patties 6 to 7 minutes on each side or until cooked through (165°F). Place cheese on patties; cover skillet just until cheese melts.

3. Serve patties on buns with mustard and lettuce.   *Makes 4 servings*

Beer Oven-Fried Chicken

1 1/3 cups pale ale
2 tablespoons buttermilk
1 1/4 cups panko bread crumbs*
1/2 cup grated Parmesan cheese
4 chicken breast cutlets
1/2 teaspoon salt
1/4 teaspoon black pepper
Chopped fresh parsley (optional)

*Panko bread crumbs are used in Japanese cooking to provide a crisp exterior to fried foods. They are coarser and lighter than ordinary bread crumbs. Panko can be found in Asian markets or in the Asian aisle of large supermarkets.

1. Preheat oven to 400°F. Stir together pale ale and buttermilk in shallow bowl. Combine bread crumbs and Parmesan in another shallow bowl.

2. Sprinkle chicken with salt and pepper. Dip in ale mixture; dredge in bread crumb mixture. Place on foil-lined baking sheet.

3. Bake 25 to 30 minutes or until chicken is no longer pink in center. Garnish with parsley.

Makes 4 servings

TIP: Chicken breast cutlets are thin slices of boneless skinless breast. If you are working with regular boneless skinless breasts, you can make cutlets by pounding them until they are about 1/4 inch thick. Split the thicker part of the breast horizontally and open it out like a book. Place it between 2 sheets of plastic wrap and pound with the flat side of a meat mallet or a rolling pin.

Beer Oven-Fried Chicken

Layered Beer Bean Dip

1 can (about 15 ounces) pinto beans, rinsed and drained
1 can (12 ounces) beer
1 1/2 cups chopped onions
3 cloves garlic, minced
2 teaspoons ground cumin
1 teaspoon dried oregano
1 teaspoon salt
1 cup guacamole
1 cup sour cream
1 cup salsa
1/2 cup chopped black olives
1/2 cup chopped green onions
1 1/2 cups (6 ounces) shredded Cheddar or Monterey Jack cheese

1. Place beans in large saucepan over medium heat. Add beer, onions, garlic, cumin, oregano and salt; simmer, stirring occasionally, 15 to 30 minutes or until no liquid remains. Remove from heat. Mash beans with potato masher or process in food processor. Set aside to cool.

2. Spread half of cooled beans in casserole or other dish that is at least 2 inches deep. Top with half of guacamole, half of sour cream, half of salsa, half of olives and half of green onions. Repeat layers and top with cheese. Serve chilled or at room temperature.

Makes 4 to 6 servings

Variation: Use refried beans instead of whole beans. Pour a 15-ounce can of your favorite refried beans into a small saucepan. Add only 6 ounces of beer and simmer for about 10 minutes. If the refried beans are not seasoned, add garlic, cumin and oregano while simmering. Let cool and proceed.

Layered Beer Bean Dip

Polska Kielbasa with Beer and Onions

⅓ cup honey mustard
⅓ cup packed dark brown sugar
1 bottle (18 ounces) brown nut ale
2 kielbasa sausages (about 2 pounds), cut into 4-inch pieces
2 onions, quartered

SLOW COOKER DIRECTIONS

Combine honey mustard and brown sugar in slow cooker. Whisk in ale. Add sausage pieces. Top with onions. Cover; cook on LOW 4 to 5 hours, stirring occasionally.

Makes 6 to 8 servings

Fiesta Bread

½ pound chorizo sausage, casings removed
½ cup chopped onion
1¼ cups all-purpose flour
1 cup cornmeal
1½ teaspoons baking soda
½ teaspoon salt
1 teaspoon cumin
1 cup Mexican beer
1 cup (4 ounces) shredded Cheddar cheese
1 can (4 ounces) diced green chiles
1 egg, beaten

1. Preheat oven to 375°F. Cook sausage and onion in medium skillet over medium-high heat until meat is no longer pink; drain fat. Combine flour, cornmeal, baking soda, salt and cumin in large bowl. Combine beer, cheese, chiles and egg in medium bowl. Stir into flour mixture until combined. Stir in sausage mixture.

2. Spread into greased 8-inch square baking pan. Bake 20 to 25 minutes or until toothpick inserted into center comes out clean. Cool 10 minutes in pan before slicing. Serve warm. Refrigerate any remaining bread. *Makes 8 servings*

Durango Chili

3 tablespoons vegetable oil, divided
1 pound lean ground beef
1 pound boneless beef top sirloin steak, cut into ½-inch cubes
2 medium onions, chopped
1 green bell pepper, chopped
4 cloves garlic, minced
2 cans (about 14 ounces each) diced tomatoes, undrained
1 can (10¾ ounces) condensed beef broth plus 1 can water
1 bottle (12 ounces) beer
2 cans (4 ounces each) diced green chiles, undrained
3 to 5 jalapeño peppers,* minced
5 tablespoons chili powder
¼ cup tomato paste
2 bay leaves
1 teaspoon salt
1 teaspoon ground cumin
½ teaspoon black pepper
2 cans (about 15 ounces each) pinto or kidney beans, rinsed and drained
  Shredded Cheddar cheese
  Sliced green onions

*Jalapeño peppers can sting and irritate the skin, so wear rubber gloves when handling peppers and do not touch your eyes.

1. Heat 1 tablespoon oil in 5-quart Dutch oven over medium-high heat. Brown ground beef, stirring to break up meat. Add cubed beef. Cook, stirring occasionally, until meat is lightly browned. Transfer to medium bowl.

2. Heat remaining 2 tablespoons oil in Dutch oven over medium heat. Add onions, bell pepper and garlic. Cook and stir until vegetables are tender. Return meat to Dutch oven. Stir in tomatoes, broth, water, beer, green chiles, jalapeño peppers, chili powder, tomato paste, bay leaves, salt, cumin and black pepper. Bring to a boil. Reduce heat and simmer, partially covered, 2 hours or until meat is very tender. Stir in beans. Simmer, uncovered, until heated through. Remove and discard bay leaves before serving. Top with cheese and green onions. *Makes 6 servings*

Bratwurst & Grilled-Onion Hoagies

1 tablespoon butter or margarine
1 large onion, thinly sliced, separated into rings
½ teaspoon paprika
¼ teaspoon salt
¼ teaspoon freshly ground black pepper
1 package JENNIE-O TURKEY STORE® Lean Turkey Bratwurst
½ cup beer, non-alcoholic beer or water
2 teaspoons olive or vegetable oil
5 hoagie or submarine sandwich rolls, split, lightly toasted
  Spicy brown mustard (optional)

Melt butter in large skillet over medium-high heat. Add onion rings; cook 3 minutes or until wilted, stirring occasionally. Sprinkle with paprika, salt and pepper. Reduce heat to medium-low; cook 15 to 20 minutes or until golden brown and tender, stirring occasionally. Meanwhile, combine bratwurst and beer or water in large saucepan. Cover and simmer 10 minutes. Pour off and discard liquid. Add oil to pan; brown bratwurst on all sides, about 6 minutes. Serve in rolls topped with onions, and, if desired, mustard.

Makes 5 servings

TIP: Both bratwurst and beer are classics of German cuisine. "Wurst" simply means sausage in German. There are hundreds of different kinds of wurst, and bratwurst is certainly one of the best and most beloved in the U.S. The sausage is made of pork, beef or veal and a mix of spices. The first recorded mention of bratwurst was in 1404 according to the German Bratwurst Museum.

Chicken and Sausage Gumbo with Beer

½ cup all-purpose flour
½ cup vegetable oil
4½ cups chicken broth
1 bottle (12 ounces) beer
3 pounds boneless skinless chicken thighs
1½ teaspoons salt, divided
½ teaspoon garlic powder
¾ teaspoon ground red pepper, divided
1 pound fully cooked andouille sausage, sliced into rounds
1 large onion, chopped
½ red bell pepper, chopped
½ green bell pepper, chopped
2 stalks celery, chopped
2 cloves garlic, minced
2 bay leaves
½ teaspoon black pepper
3 cups hot cooked rice
½ cup sliced green onions
1 teaspoon filé powder (optional)

1. Stir together flour and oil in Dutch oven. Cook over medium-low heat, stirring frequently, 20 minutes or until mixture is the color of caramel. (Once mixture begins to darken, watch carefully to avoid burning.)

2. Meanwhile, heat broth and beer in medium saucepan to a simmer. Keep warm over low heat. Season chicken with ½ teaspoon salt, garlic powder and ¼ teaspoon ground red pepper.

3. Add chicken, sausage, onion, bell peppers, celery, garlic, bay leaves, remaining 1 teaspoon salt, black pepper and remaining ½ teaspoon ground red pepper to Dutch oven. Stir well. Ladle in hot broth mixture, stirring constantly to prevent lumps. Bring to a simmer. Cover and simmer over low heat 1 to 2 hours. Remove and discard bay leaves. Spoon ½ cup rice into bowls and ladle gumbo over top. Sprinkle with green onions and filé powder, if desired, before serving. *Makes 6 servings*

Chicken and Vegetable Satay with Peanut Sauce

1½ pounds boneless skinless chicken thighs, cut into chunks
⅔ cup Thai beer, divided
3 tablespoons packed dark brown sugar, divided
1 tablespoon plus 2 teaspoons lime juice, divided
3 cloves garlic, minced, divided
1¼ teaspoons curry powder, divided
½ cup coconut milk
½ cup chunky peanut butter, preferably natural
1 tablespoon fish sauce
3 tablespoons peanut oil, divided
¼ cup finely chopped onion
24 medium mushrooms, stems trimmed
4 green onions, cut into 24 (1-inch) pieces
Hot cooked noodles or rice (optional)

1. Combine chicken, ⅓ cup beer, 1 tablespoon sugar, 1 tablespoon lime juice, two thirds of garlic and 1 teaspoon curry powder in large resealable food storage bag. Refrigerate 2 hours, turning occasionally.

2. For peanut sauce, combine remaining ⅓ cup beer, remaining 2 tablespoons sugar, remaining 2 teaspoons lime juice, coconut milk, peanut butter and fish sauce in medium bowl. Heat 1 tablespoon oil in small saucepan over medium-high heat. Add onion and remaining one third of garlic; cook 2 to 3 minutes or until starting to soften. Add remaining ¼ teaspoon curry powder and cook 15 seconds. Stir in coconut milk mixture. Reduce heat to medium; simmer, stirring often, until thickened, about 15 minutes. Keep warm.

3. Prepare grill for direct cooking. Remove chicken from marinade; discard marinade. Thread chicken, mushrooms and green onions onto 8 skewers. Brush skewers with remaining 2 tablespoons oil. Grill 8 to 10 minutes, turning occasionally, until chicken is cooked through. Serve over noodles with peanut sauce. *Makes 4 servings*

Texas Smoked BBQ Brisket

½ cup prepared barbecue seasoning

2 tablespoons ground chili powder

1 (5 to 7 pound) beef brisket, trimmed with a layer of fat (center flat portion)

1 cup *Frank's® RedHot® Chile 'n Lime™* Hot Sauce or *Frank's® RedHot®* Cayenne Pepper Sauce

1½ cups beer or non-alcoholic malt beverage

1 cup *Cattlemen's®* Authentic Smoke House Barbecue Sauce or *Cattlemen's®* Award Winning Classic Barbecue Sauce

¼ cup butter

1. Combine barbecue seasoning and chili powder. Rub mixture thoroughly into beef. Place meat, fat-side up, into disposable foil pan. Cover and refrigerate 1 to 3 hours. Just before using, prepare mop sauce by combining *Chile 'n Lime™* Hot Sauce and 1 cup beer; set aside.

2. Prepare grill for indirect cooking over medium-low heat (250°F). If desired, toss soaked wood chips over coals or heat source. Place pan with meat in center of grill over indirect heat. Cover grill. Cook meat, over low heat 6 to 7 hours until meat is very tender (190°F internal temperature). Baste with mop sauce once an hour.

3. Combine barbecue sauce, butter and remaining ½ cup beer. Simmer 5 minutes until slightly thickened. Slice meat and serve with sauce. *Makes 10 to 12 servings*

Tip: To easily slice meat, cut against the grain using an electric knife.

Prep Time: 15 minutes • **Cook Time:** 7 hours • **Marinate Time:** 1 hour

Guadalajara Beef

    1 bottle (12 ounces) dark beer
    ¼ cup soy sauce
    3 cloves garlic, minced
    1 teaspoon ground cumin
    1 teaspoon chili powder
    ½ teaspoon ground red pepper
    1 beef flank steak (about 1 pound)
    6 medium red, yellow or green bell peppers, cut into quarters
    8 (6- to 8-inch) flour tortillas
       Sour cream
       Salsa

1. Combine beer, soy sauce, garlic, cumin, chili powder and red pepper in large resealable food storage bag; knead bag to combine. Add beef and seal. Refrigerate up to 24 hours, turning occasionally.

2. Prepare grill for direct cooking. Remove beef from marinade; discard marinade. Place beef on grid over medium heat. Grill, uncovered, 17 to 21 minutes for medium rare to medium (145°F) or until desired doneness, turning once. Grill bell peppers 7 to 10 minutes or until tender, turning once.

3. Cut steak across the grain into thin slices. Serve in tortillas with bell peppers, sour cream and salsa.

Makes 4 servings

Sesame Hoisin Beer-Can Chicken

1 can (12 ounces) beer, divided
½ cup hoisin sauce
2 tablespoons honey
1 tablespoon soy sauce
1 teaspoon chili-garlic sauce
½ teaspoon dark sesame oil
1 chicken (3½ to 4 pounds), rinsed and patted dry

1. Prepare grill for indirect cooking. Combine 2 tablespoons beer, hoisin sauce, honey, soy sauce, chili-garlic sauce and sesame oil in small bowl. With your fingers, gently loosen skin of chicken over breast meat, legs and thighs. Spoon some hoisin mixture into cavity and under skin. Pour off beer until can is two-thirds full. Hold chicken upright with opening of cavity pointing down. Insert beer can into cavity.

2. Stand chicken upright on can over drip pan. Spread legs slightly to help support chicken. Cover; grill over indirect medium heat 30 minutes. Brush chicken with remaining hoisin mixture. Cover; grill 45 to 60 minutes or until chicken is cooked through (165°F). Use metal tongs to lift chicken to cutting board. Let rest, standing up, 5 minutes. Carefully remove beer can and discard. Carve chicken and serve. *Makes 2 to 4 servings*

Sesame Hoisin Beer-Can Chicken

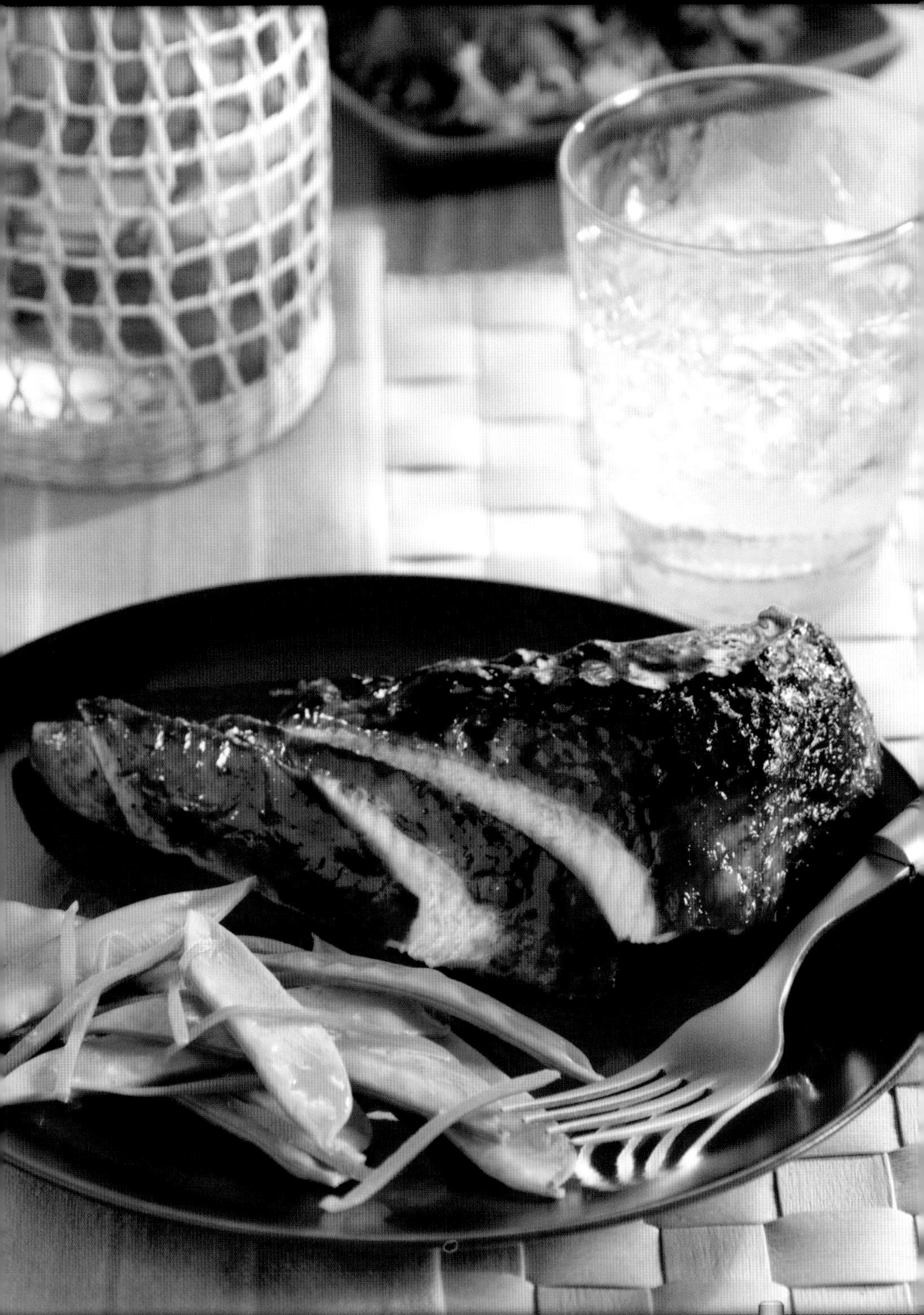

Farmers' Market Grilled Chowder

1 ear corn
1 large potato
1 zucchini, cut lengthwise into 1/4-inch-thick slices
   Nonstick cooking spray
1 tablespoon butter
1/2 cup chopped onion
2 tablespoons all-purpose flour
1/2 teaspoon salt
1/2 teaspoon dried thyme
1/8 teaspoon white pepper
1 cup wheat beer
1 cup milk
1/2 cup (2 ounces) shredded sharp Cheddar cheese

1. Prepare grill for direct cooking. Remove husks and silk from corn. Cut potato in half lengthwise. Grill corn and potato, covered, over medium heat 20 minutes or until corn is beginning to brown and potato is tender, turning to cook evenly. Cut kernels from cob. Cut potato into bite-size pieces.

2. Spray both sides of zucchini with cooking spray. Grill, uncovered, 4 minutes or until tender, turning once. Cut into bite-size pieces.

3. Melt butter in large saucepan over medium heat. Add onion; cook and stir 5 minutes or until tender. Stir in flour, salt, thyme and pepper. Cook and stir about 1 minute.

4. Whisk beer and milk into flour mixture. Cook and stir over medium heat until mixture comes to a simmer; simmer 1 minute. Stir in corn, potato, zucchini and cheese. Reduce heat to low; simmer, stirring constantly, until cheese is melted and mixture is hot.

Makes 4 servings

Grilled Skirt Steak Fajitas

1 1/2 pounds skirt steak
1/2 cup pale ale
3 tablespoons lime juice
1 teaspoon ground cumin
2 tablespoons olive oil
1 cup thinly sliced red onion
1 cup thinly sliced red and green bell peppers
2 cloves garlic, minced
3 plum tomatoes, quartered
1 tablespoon soy sauce
3/4 teaspoon salt
1/4 teaspoon black pepper
8 (7-inch) flour tortillas, warmed
Avocado slices, salsa and sour cream (optional)

1. Combine steak, pale ale, lime juice and cumin in resealable food storage bag. Seal bag; turn to coat. Refrigerate 2 hours, turning occasionally.

2. Meanwhile, heat oil in large nonstick skillet over medium-high heat. Add onion; cook and stir 2 to 3 minutes or until starting to soften. Stir in bell peppers; cook, stirring occasionally, until softened, 7 to 8 minutes. Add garlic; cook and stir 1 minute. Add tomatoes; cook 2 minutes or until just beginning to soften. Add soy sauce; cook 1 minute. Keep warm.

3. Prepare grill for direct cooking over medium-high heat.

4. Remove steak from marinade; discard marinade. Sprinkle with salt and pepper. Grill 4 to 6 minutes on each side for medium-rare (145°F). Transfer to cutting board; cut across grain into thin slices.

5. Fill tortillas with steak and vegetables. Top with avocado slices, salsa and sour cream, if desired. *Makes 4 servings*

Brats 'n' Beer

1 can or bottle (12 ounces) light-colored beer
4 bratwurst (about 1 pound)
1 sweet or Spanish onion, thinly sliced and separated into rings
1 tablespoon olive oil
¼ teaspoon salt
¼ teaspoon black pepper
4 hot dog rolls

1. Prepare grill for direct cooking.

2. Pour beer into heavy, medium saucepan with ovenproof handle. (If not ovenproof, wrap heavy-duty foil around handle.) Place saucepan on grill.

3. Pierce bratwurst with knife; add to beer. Simmer, uncovered, over medium heat 15 minutes, turning once during cooking.

4. Place onion rings on heavy-duty foil. Drizzle with oil; sprinkle with salt and pepper. Fold sides of foil over rings to enclose. Place packets on grill. Grill, uncovered, 10 to 15 minutes or until onion rings are tender.

5. Transfer bratwurst to grill. Remove saucepan from grill; discard beer. Grill bratwurst 10 minutes or until browned and cooked through, turning once during grilling.

6. Place bratwurst in rolls. Top with onions.

Makes 4 servings

TIP: Don't forget the condiments when serving brats or other sausages. In addition to Dijon or yellow mustard, you may want to offer honey mustard or even one of the flavored mustards now available. Try mustard seasoned with hot peppers, spice or bourbon. Fresh tomato wedges or giardiniera are also nice options.

Cajun Chicken Nuggets & Grilled Fruit

½ cup beer or non-alcoholic malt beverage
¼ cup *French's*® Spicy Brown Mustard
2 tablespoons oil
1 pound boneless skinless chicken breasts, cut into 1½-inch pieces
¾ cup plain dry bread crumbs
1 tablespoon plus 1 teaspoon prepared Cajun seasoning blend
1 pineapple, peeled, cored and cut into ½-inch-thick rings
2 peaches, cut into 1-inch-thick wedges

1. Combine beer, mustard and oil in large bowl. Add chicken pieces; toss to coat evenly. Cover; marinate in refrigerator 20 minutes.

2. Preheat oven to 350°F. Coat baking sheet with nonstick cooking spray. Combine bread crumbs and Cajun seasoning in pie plate. Remove chicken from marinade; roll in bread crumb mixture to coat. Discard any remaining marinade. Place chicken on prepared baking sheet. Bake 20 minutes or until light golden brown and no longer pink in center, turning once. Remove to serving plate.

3. Coat fruit with nonstick cooking spray. Place fruit on oiled grid. Grill 5 to 8 minutes over medium heat until just tender. Serve with chicken nuggets and Peachy Mustard Glaze (recipe follows). *Makes 4 servings*

Prep Time: 20 minutes • **Marinate Time:** 20 minutes • **Cook Time:** 20 minutes

Peachy Mustard Glaze

¾ cup peach preserves
¼ cup *French's*® Classic Yellow® Mustard
2 tablespoons orange juice

Microwave preserves in small bowl on HIGH (100%) 2 minutes or until melted, stirring once. Stir in mustard and juice. *Makes 1 cup glaze*

Prep Time: 5 minutes

Cajun BBQ Beer-Can Chicken

4 (12-ounce) cans beer or non-alcoholic malt beverage
1½ cups *Cattlemen's®* Award Winning Classic Barbecue Sauce
¾ cup Cajun spice or Southwest seasoning blend
3 whole chickens (3 to 4 pounds each)
12 sprigs fresh thyme

CAJUN BBQ SAUCE

1 cup *Cattlemen's®* Award Winning Classic Barbecue Sauce
½ cup beer or non-alcoholic malt beverage
¼ cup butter
1 tablespoon Cajun spice or Southwest seasoning blend

1. Combine 1 can beer, 1½ cups barbecue sauce and ½ cup spice blend. Following manufacturer's instructions, fill marinade injection needle with marinade. Inject chickens in several places at least 1-inch deep. Place chickens into resealable plastic food storage bags. Pour any remaining marinade over chickens. Seal bag; marinate in refrigerator 1 to 3 hours or overnight.

2. Meanwhile prepare Cajun BBQ Sauce: In saucepan, combine 1 cup barbecue sauce, ½ cup beer, butter and 1 tablespoon spice blend. Simmer 5 minutes. Refrigerate and warm just before serving.

3. Open remaining cans of beer. Spill out about ½ cup beer from each can. Using can opener, punch several holes in tops of cans. Spoon about 1 tablespoon additional spice blend and 4 sprigs thyme into each can. Place 1 can upright into cavity of each chicken, arranging legs forward so chicken stands upright.

4. Place chickens upright over indirect heat on barbecue grill. Cook on a covered grill on medium-high (350°F), about 1½ hours until thigh meat registers 180°F internal temperature. (Cover chickens with foil if they become too brown while cooking.) Let stand 10 minutes before serving. Using tongs, carefully remove cans from chicken. Cut into quarters to serve. Serve with Cajun BBQ Sauce.   *Makes 12 servings*

Prep Time: 20 minutes • **Cook Time:** 1½ hours • **Marinate Time:** 1 hour or overnight

Hickory Beef Kabobs

1 pound boneless beef top sirloin or tenderloin steaks, cut into 1¼-inch pieces
2 ears fresh corn,* shucked, silk removed and cut into 1-inch pieces
1 red or green bell pepper, cut into 1-inch squares
1 small red onion, cut into ½-inch wedges
½ cup beer
½ cup chili sauce
1 teaspoon dry mustard
2 cloves garlic, minced
3 cups hot cooked rice
¼ cup chopped fresh parsley

*Four small ears frozen corn, thawed, can be substituted for fresh corn.

1. Place beef, corn, bell pepper and onion in large resealable food storage bag. Combine beer, chili sauce, mustard and garlic in small bowl; pour over beef and vegetables. Seal bag; turn to coat. Marinate in refrigerator at least 1 hour or up to 8 hours, turning occasionally.

2. Cover 1½ cups hickory chips with cold water; soak 20 minutes. Meanwhile, prepare grill for direct cooking.

3. Drain beef and vegetables; reserve marinade. Alternately thread beef and vegetables onto 4 (12-inch) metal skewers. Brush with reserved marinade.

4. Drain hickory chips; sprinkle over coals. Grill kabobs, uncovered, over medium heat 5 minutes. Brush with reserved marinade; turn and brush again. Discard remaining marinade. Continue to grill 5 to 7 minutes for medium or until desired doneness.

5. Combine rice and parsley; serve kabobs over rice mixture.   *Makes 4 servings*

Grilled Chicken Breast and Beer-Braised Onion Burgers

4 boneless skinless chicken breasts, pounded slightly
1/2 cup lager
3 tablespoons Dijon mustard
1 tablespoon paprika
1 tablespoon olive oil
2 cloves garlic, minced
1 teaspoon dried basil
3/4 teaspoon salt
1/4 teaspoon black pepper
4 English muffins, toasted
    Beer-Braised Onions (recipe follows)

1. Place chicken in large resealable food storage bag. Combine lager, mustard, paprika, oil, garlic and basil in small bowl. Pour over chicken. Seal bag; turn to coat. Refrigerate 2 hours, turning occasionally.

2. Prepare grill for direct cooking.

3. Remove chicken from marinade; discard marinade. Lightly oil grill grid. Sprinkle chicken with salt and pepper. Place chicken directly over heat source. Grill, covered, over medium-high heat 4 to 6 minutes per side or until no longer pink in center.

4. Serve on English muffins with Beer-Braised Onions.

Makes 4 servings

Beer-Braised Onions

1 tablespoon unsalted butter
1 1/2 cups thinly sliced red onions (about 1 medium onion)
2 tablespoons sugar
2 tablespoons lager
1 tablespoon balsamic vinegar
1/4 teaspoon salt

Melt butter in medium nonstick skillet over medium heat. Add onions and sugar; cook, stirring occasionally, until onion is soft but not brown, 5 to 7 minutes. Stir in lager, vinegar and salt; cook 1 minute or until liquid evaporates.

Makes 1/2 cup

Spicy Smoked Beef Ribs

Wood chunks or chips for smoking
4 to 6 pounds beef back ribs, cut into 3 to 4 rib pieces
Black pepper
1⅓ cups barbecue sauce
2 teaspoons hot pepper sauce or Szechwan chili sauce
Beer at room temperature
Grilled corn on the cob (optional)

1. Prepare grill for indirect grilling. Soak 4 wood chunks or several handfuls of wood chips in water; drain.

2. Spread ribs on baking sheet or tray; season with pepper. Combine barbecue sauce and hot pepper sauce in small bowl. Brush ribs with half of sauce. Marinate in refrigerator 30 minutes to 1 hour.

3. Arrange low coals on each side of rectangular metal or foil drip pan. (Since the ribs have been brushed with sauce before cooking, low heat is needed to keep them moist.) Pour in beer to fill pan half full. Add soaked wood (all the chunks or part of the chips) to fire.

4. Oil hot grid to help prevent sticking. Place ribs on grid, meaty side up, directly above drip pan. Grill, covered, over low heat about 1 hour, brushing remaining sauce over ribs 2 or 3 times during cooking. (If grill has thermometer, maintain cooking temperature between 250°F to 275°F.) Add briquets after 30 minutes, or as needed to maintain constant temperature. Add more soaked wood chips after 30 minutes, if necessary. Serve with grilled corn on the cob, if desired. *Makes 4 to 6 servings*

TIP: When grilling ribs or other meats that require a long cooking time, be careful not to burn the barbecue sauce. Sweet sauces especially can char very easily. Keep the heat low and consider brushing on the sauce towards the end of cooking time if it seems to be browning too quickly.

Spicy Smoked Beef Ribs

Grilled Chicken with Chili Beer Baste

2 tablespoons vegetable oil
1 small onion, chopped
1 clove garlic, minced
½ cup ketchup
2 chipotle peppers in adobo sauce, minced
2 tablespoons brown sugar
2 teaspoons chili powder
1 teaspoon dry mustard
½ teaspoon salt
½ teaspoon black pepper
3 bottles (12 ounces each) pilsner, divided
½ cup tomato juice
¼ cup Worcestershire sauce
1 tablespoon lemon juice
2 whole chickens (about 3½ pounds each), cut up

1. To make Chili Beer Baste, heat oil in large saucepan over medium heat. Add onion and garlic; cook and stir until onion is tender. Combine ketchup, chipotle peppers, brown sugar, chili powder, mustard, salt and black pepper in medium bowl. Add 1 bottle pilsner, tomato juice, Worcestershire sauce and lemon juice; whisk until well blended. Pour mixture into saucepan with onion and garlic. Bring to a simmer; cook until sauce is thickened slightly and reduced to about 2 cups. Let cool. Refrigerate overnight.

2. Place chicken pieces in 2 large resealable food storage bags. Pour remaining 2 bottles pilsner over chickens; seal bags. Refrigerate 8 hours or overnight.

3. Prepare grill for direct cooking. Remove chickens from pilsner; discard pilsner. Place chickens on grid over medium heat. Grill 15 to 20 minutes, turning occasionally.

4. Remove Chili Beer Baste from refrigerator; set aside 1 cup. Continue grilling chicken, basting frequently, 10 minutes or until cooked through (165°F). Warm reserved Chili Beer Baste and serve with chicken. *Makes 8 servings*

Mole Chicken

3 tablespoons vegetable oil
1 chicken (about 4 pounds), cut into 8 pieces
1 medium onion, chopped
1 green bell pepper, diced
3 cloves garlic, chopped
2 tablespoons chili powder
2 teaspoons ground cumin
1/2 teaspoon ground cinnamon
1 can (about 14 ounces) diced tomatoes, undrained
1 cup chicken broth
1 cup dark Mexican beer
1/4 cup raisins
2 chipotle peppers in adobo sauce, chopped
2 tablespoons peanut butter
1 tablespoon sugar
1 teaspoon salt
2 squares (1 ounce each) unsweetened chocolate, chopped
   Hot cooked rice
   Sour cream and chopped fresh cilantro (optional)

1. Heat oil in large skillet over medium heat; add chicken pieces in batches. Brown on all sides. Transfer chicken to large baking pan or casserole and set aside.

2. Stir together onion, bell pepper and garlic in same skillet. Cook and stir about 5 minutes or until vegetables are softened. Stir in chili powder, cumin and cinnamon; cook 5 minutes. Add tomatoes, broth, beer, raisins, chipotle peppers, peanut butter, sugar and salt. Bring to a simmer and cook 20 minutes, stirring often. Pour into blender or food processor. Add chocolate; process until smooth.

3. Preheat oven to 350°F. Pour sauce over browned chicken pieces. Cover pan loosely with foil; bake 45 minutes or until chicken is cooked through (165°F) and sauce is bubbling.

4. Serve with rice. Garnish with dollop of sour cream and cilantro. *Makes 4 servings*

Tip: This recipe makes plenty of sauce. Drizzle extra sauce around the plate or serve over side dishes.

Rio Grande Ribs

4 pounds country-style pork ribs, trimmed of all visible fat
   Salt, to taste
   Black pepper, to taste
1 jar (16 ounces) picante sauce
½ cup beer, nonalcoholic malt beverage or beef broth
¼ cup *Frank's® RedHot®* Cayenne Pepper Sauce
1 teaspoon chili powder
2 cups *French's®* French Fried Onions

1. Season ribs with salt and pepper. Broil ribs 6 inches from heat on rack in broiler pan for 10 minutes or until well-browned, turning once. Place ribs in the slow cooker. Combine picante sauce, beer, *Frank's RedHot* Sauce and chili powder in small bowl. Pour mixture over top.

2. Cover and cook on LOW for 6 hours or on HIGH for 3 hours or until ribs are tender. Transfer ribs to serving platter; keep warm. Skim fat from liquid.

3. Turn the slow cooker to HIGH. Add *1 cup* French Fried Onions to the stoneware. Cook 10 to 15 minutes or until slightly thickened. Spoon sauce over ribs and sprinkle with remaining *1 cup* French Fried Onions. Splash on more *Frank's RedHot* Sauce to taste.

Makes 6 servings

Beer-Brined Chicken

4 cups water
3 cups stout
2 cups apple juice
1/2 cup kosher salt plus 1/2 teaspoon, divided
1/2 cup packed light brown sugar
1 teaspoon paprika
1 sprig fresh rosemary plus 1 tablespoon chopped, divided
1 bay leaf
1 chicken (3 1/2 to 4 pounds)
1/4 cup butter (1/2 stick), melted
1/4 teaspoon black pepper

1. Combine water, stout, apple juice, 1/2 cup salt, sugar, paprika, rosemary sprig and bay leaf in large Dutch oven. Stir until salt and sugar are dissolved. Add chicken; cover. Refrigerate 2 to 4 hours.

2. Preheat oven to 425°F. Remove chicken from brine; discard brine. Pat chicken dry; tie drumsticks together to maintain best shape. Place on rack in roasting pan. Cover loosely with foil; roast 45 minutes.

3. Remove foil. Combine butter, chopped rosemary, remaining 1/2 teaspoon salt and pepper in small bowl; brush all over chicken. Continue roasting until juices run clear and meat thermometer reads 165°F. If chicken begins to get too dark, cover loosely with foil.

4. Let stand 10 minutes before carving.   *Makes 2 to 4 servings*

Beer-Brined Chicken

Mussels in Beer Broth

2 tablespoons olive oil
1/3 cup chopped shallots
4 cloves garlic, minced
1 can (about 14 ounces) Italian-style diced tomatoes, undrained
1/4 cup chopped fresh parsley
1 tablespoon chopped fresh thyme
1/2 teaspoon salt
1/4 teaspoon red pepper flakes
2 cups pale ale
3 pounds mussels, scrubbed and debearded
French bread (optional)

Heat oil in large saucepan or Dutch oven. Add shallots and garlic; cook and stir 3 minutes or until tender. Stir in tomatoes, parsley, thyme, salt and red pepper flakes. Add pale ale; bring to a boil. Add mussels; cover. Reduce heat and simmer 5 to 7 minutes or until shells open. Serve with French bread, if desired.   *Makes 4 servings*

TIP: Many mussels are farm-raised and only need to be rinsed well in cold water before cooking. Discard any mussels that are chipped or broken or do not close tightly. Scrub off any barnacles, sand or grit on wild mussels and remove the beard. The beard is a collection of tough fibers that the mussel uses to attach itself to a rock or other object in the water. To remove it, grasp tightly with a paper towel and pull towards the hinged end of the shell.

Spice-Rubbed Beef Brisket

2 cups hickory chips
1 teaspoon salt
1 teaspoon paprika
1 teaspoon chili powder
1 teaspoon garlic pepper
1 beef brisket (3 to 3½ pounds)
¼ cup beer
1 tablespoon Worcestershire sauce
1 tablespoon balsamic vinegar
1 teaspoon olive oil
¼ teaspoon dry mustard
6 ears corn, cut into 2-inch pieces
12 small new potatoes
6 carrots, cut into 2-inch pieces
2 green bell peppers, cut into 2-inch squares
¼ cup plus 2 tablespoons water
¼ cup plus 2 tablespoons lemon juice
1½ teaspoons Italian seasoning

1. Cover hickory chips with water and soak 30 minutes. Prepare grill for indirect grilling. Bank briquets on either side of water-filled drip pan.

2. Combine salt, paprika, chili powder and garlic pepper in small bowl. Rub spice mixture onto both sides of brisket; loosely cover with foil and set aside. Combine beer, Worcestershire sauce, vinegar, oil and dry mustard in small bowl; set aside.

3. Drain hickory chips; sprinkle ½ cup over coals. Place brisket on grid directly over drip pan. Grill, covered, over medium coals 30 minutes. Baste with reserved beer mixture. Continue grilling, turning over every 30 minutes, 3 hours or until meat thermometer reaches 160°F when inserted into thickest part of brisket. (Add 4 to 9 briquets and ¼ cup hickory chips to each side of fire every hour.)

4. Meanwhile, thread corn, potatoes, carrots and bell peppers onto metal skewers. Combine water, lemon juice and Italian seasoning in small bowl; brush onto vegetables. Grill vegetables with brisket 20 to 25 minutes or until tender, turning once.

5. Remove brisket to cutting board; tent loosely with foil. Let stand 10 minutes before carving. Serve with vegetable kabobs. *Makes 12 servings*

Irish Lamb Stew

½ cup all-purpose flour
2 teaspoons salt, divided
½ teaspoon pepper, divided
3 pounds boneless lamb stew meat, cut into 1½-inch cubes
3 tablespoons vegetable oil
1 cup chopped onion
1 can (about 15 ounces) stout
1 teaspoon sugar
1 teaspoon dried thyme
1 pound small new potatoes, quartered
1 pound carrots, peeled and cut into ½-inch pieces
½ cup water
1 cup frozen peas
¼ cup chopped fresh parsley

1. Mix flour with 1 teaspoon salt and ¼ teaspoon pepper in large bowl. Toss lamb pieces in flour mixture and shake off excess. Heat oil over medium heat in Dutch oven. Working in batches, brown lamb pieces on all sides, about 7 minutes per batch. Transfer browned lamb to bowl.

2. Add onions and ¼ cup stout to Dutch oven; cook over medium heat 10 minutes, scraping up any browned bits from bottom of Dutch oven. Return lamb to Dutch oven and stir in remaining stout, sugar, thyme, remaining 1 teaspoon salt and ¼ teaspoon pepper. If needed, add enough water so that liquid just covers lamb. Cover; simmer 1½ hours or until lamb is tender.

3. Add potatoes, carrots and water. Cook, covered, 30 minutes or until vegetables are tender. Stir in peas and parsley; simmer 5 to 10 minutes before serving.

Makes 8 servings

Boston Brown Bread Muffins

½ cup rye flour
½ cup whole wheat flour
½ cup yellow cornmeal
1½ teaspoons baking soda
¾ teaspoon salt
1 cup buttermilk
⅓ cup packed dark brown sugar
⅓ cup molasses
⅓ cup dark beer
1 egg
1 cup golden raisins
  Softened cream cheese

1. Preheat oven to 400°F. Grease 12 (2⅔-inch) muffin cups or line with paper baking cups.

2. Combine rye flour, wheat flour, cornmeal, baking soda and salt in large bowl. Combine buttermilk, brown sugar, molasses, beer and egg in medium bowl. Add to flour mixture along with raisins; stir until combined.

3. Fill prepared muffin cups. Bake 15 minutes or until toothpick inserted into center comes out clean. Serve with cream cheese. *Makes 12 muffins*

TIP: Baking with beer may at first seem like an unusual idea, but the yeast and bubbles in beer can lighten the texture of baked goods as well as add a malty flavor that works well in many recipes. Be careful of overly bitter beers that are heavy on hops. The bitterness can be concentrated and exaggerated in the end product.

Beer-Braised Osso Bucco

½ cup all-purpose flour
1 teaspoon salt
½ teaspoon black pepper
4 veal shanks (about 3 pounds), cut into 1-inch rounds
3 tablespoons canola oil
3 carrots, chopped
3 celery stalks, chopped
1 large onion, sliced
2 cloves garlic, minced
1 bottle (12 ounces) beer
2 tablespoons tomato paste
2 cups beef broth
1 bay leaf
  Grated peel of 1 lemon
  Salt and black pepper
  Hot mashed potatoes or cooked polenta
  Chopped fresh parsley

1. Preheat oven to 325°F. Combine flour, salt and pepper in medium bowl. Add veal shanks and turn to coat with flour mixture.

2. Heat oil in large ovenproof saucepan or Dutch oven over medium-high heat. Brown veal shanks in batches 4 to 6 minutes. Transfer to plate. Reduce heat to medium. Add carrots, celery and onion; cook and stir about 5 minutes or until softened. Add garlic; cook and stir 1 minute. Stir in beer and tomato paste. Cook, scraping browned bits from bottom of pan. Return shanks to pan.

3. Add broth, bay leaf, lemon peel, salt and pepper to saucepan. Bring to a boil over high heat. Cover; transfer to oven. Bake 2½ to 3 hours or until veal is fork-tender. Remove shanks to platter and keep warm. Boil sauce until reduced to about 2 cups. Remove and discard bay leaf. Serve shanks in soup bowls with mashed potatoes and sauce. Sprinkle with chopped parsley. *Makes 4 servings*

Steamed Maryland Crabs

2 bottles (12 ounces each) beer
2 cups cider vinegar or white vinegar
2 dozen live Maryland blue crabs
1 cup seafood seasoning

1. Pour beer and vinegar into large stockpot. Place steaming rack in bottom of pot. Place half of crabs on rack. Sprinkle half of seasoning over crabs. Repeat layering with remaining crabs and seasoning.

2. Cover; cook over high heat until liquid begins to steam. Steam about 25 minutes or until crabs turn red and meat is white. Remove crabs to large serving platter with tongs.

3. To serve, cover table with disposable paper cloth or newspaper. To pick crabs, place each crab on its back. With thumb or knife point, pry off "apron" flap (the "pull tab"-looking shell in the center) and discard.

4. Lift off top shell and discard. With knife edge, scrape off 6 gills (lungs) on either side of the body.

5. The yellow or reddish-brown material behind the mouth area is the fat, heart and/or the crab roe and is edible. Discard the mouth area.

6. Hold crab at each side; break apart at center. Remove membrane cover with knife, exposing large chunks of meat; remove with fingers or knife.

7. Crack claws with mallet or knife handle to get to meat.   *Makes 4 servings*

Note: Two dozen crabs will yield about 2½ cups cleaned crab meat.

Bacon and Cheese Rarebit

12 slices bacon
1 small loaf (8 ounces) egg bread or challah, cut into 6 (1-inch-thick) slices
1½ tablespoons butter
½ cup light-colored beer
2 teaspoons Worcestershire sauce
2 teaspoons Dijon mustard
⅛ teaspoon ground red pepper
2 cups (8 ounces) shredded American cheese
1½ cups (6 ounces) shredded sharp Cheddar cheese
12 large slices tomato

1. Cook bacon in large skillet over medium-high heat about 7 minutes or until crisp. Remove bacon to paper towels.

2. Toast bread slices until golden brown. Cover and keep warm.

3. Preheat broiler. Melt butter in double boiler over simmering water. Stir in beer, Worcestershire sauce, mustard and red pepper; heat through.

4. Gradually add cheeses, stirring constantly until cheeses are melted. Remove from heat; cover and keep warm.

5. Arrange toast on greased or foil-lined baking pan. Top each with 2 tomato slices and 2 bacon slices. Spoon about ¼ cup cheese sauce on top. Broil 4 to 5 inches from heat 2 to 3 minutes or until cheese begins to brown. Transfer to individual serving plates. Serve immediately.

Makes 6 servings

French Onion Soup

¼ cup (½ stick) butter
6 cups thinly sliced onions
1 teaspoon sugar
4 cups beef broth
1 bottle (12 ounces) stout
1 teaspoon salt
½ teaspoon dried thyme
½ teaspoon black pepper
4 slices French bread
4 slices Gruyère cheese

1. Heat butter in 4-quart Dutch oven over medium-low heat; add onions. Cook, stirring occasionally, until onions are very soft, about 30 minutes. Add sugar; continue cooking, stirring often, until onions are deep golden brown, about 15 minutes.

2. Add broth, stout, salt, thyme and pepper. Increase heat to medium-high; bring mixture to a boil. Reduce heat to low; simmer 30 minutes.

3. Meanwhile, preheat oven to 350°F. Place bread on baking sheet. Bake 15 minutes, turning once, until toasted.

4. Preheat broiler. Spoon soup into ovenproof soup bowls. Place bread slice in each bowl; top with cheese. Broil about 4 inches from heat until cheese is melted.

Makes 4 servings

TIP: For classic French Onion Soup it's important to cook the onions for a long time over low heat. This helps caramelize the onions and bring out their natural sugars. While 6 cups of onions may sound like a lot (and it is a lot of onions to slice!), they will shrink down to a manageable size after cooking.

Irish Stout Chicken

2 tablespoons vegetable oil
1 medium onion, chopped
2 cloves garlic, minced
1 whole chicken (3 to 4 pounds), cut up
5 carrots, cut into bite-sized pieces
2 parsnips, cut into bite-sized pieces
1 teaspoon dried thyme
¾ teaspoon salt
½ teaspoon black pepper
¾ cup stout
½ pound button mushrooms
¾ cup peas

1. Heat oil in large Dutch oven over medium heat. Add onion and garlic; cook and stir 3 minutes or until tender. Remove to small bowl.

2. Add chicken in single layer to Dutch oven. Cook over medium-high heat 5 minutes per side or until lightly browned.

3. Add onion, garlic, carrots, parsnips, thyme, salt and pepper to Dutch oven. Pour in stout; bring to a boil over high heat. Reduce heat to low. Cover; simmer 35 minutes.

4. Add mushrooms and peas to Dutch oven. Cover; cook 10 minutes.

5. Uncover; increase heat to medium. Cook 10 minutes or until sauce is slightly thickened and chicken is cooked through (165°F). *Makes 4 servings*

Irish Stout Chicken

Fish & Chips

¾ cup all-purpose flour
½ cup flat beer
   Vegetable oil
4 medium russet potatoes, each cut into 8 wedges
   Salt
1 egg, separated
1 pound cod fillets (about 6 to 8 small fillets)
   Malt vinegar and lemon wedges (optional)

1. Combine flour, beer and 2 teaspoons oil in small bowl. Cover; refrigerate 1 to 2 hours.

2. Pour 2 inches oil into Dutch oven or heavy skillet. Heat over medium heat to 365°F. Fry potato wedges in batches 4 to 6 minutes or until browned, turning once. (Do not crowd pan. Allow oil to regain temperature between batches.) Drain on paper towels; sprinkle lightly with salt. Reserve oil to fry cod.

3. Stir egg yolk into reserved flour mixture. Beat egg white in medium bowl with electric mixer at medium-high speed until soft peaks form. Fold egg white into flour mixture.

4. Return oil to 365°F. Dip fish into batter in batches. Fry 4 to 6 minutes or until batter is crispy and brown and fish begins to flake easily when tested with fork, turning once. Drain on paper towels. Serve immediately with potato wedges, vinegar and lemon wedges, if desired.   *Makes 4 servings*

Chocolate Stout Cake

2 cups all-purpose flour
¾ cup unsweetened cocoa
1 teaspoon baking soda
¼ teaspoon salt
¾ cup (1½ sticks) butter, softened
1 cup packed light brown sugar
½ cup granulated sugar
1 teaspoon vanilla
3 eggs
1 cup stout, at room temperature
Cream Cheese Frosting (recipe follows)

1. Preheat oven to 350°F. Spray 13×9-inch baking pan with nonstick cooking spray. Combine flour, cocoa, baking soda and salt in medium bowl.

2. Beat butter, brown sugar and granulated sugar in large bowl with electric mixer at medium speed until light and fluffy. Beat in vanilla. Add eggs, 1 at a time, beating after each addition.

3. Add flour mixture alternately with stout, beating after each addition. Pour batter into prepared pan.

4. Bake 35 to 40 minutes or until toothpick inserted into center comes out clean. Cool on wire rack.

5. Prepare Cream Cheese Frosting; spread over cake.   *Makes 12 servings*

Cream Cheese Frosting

¼ cup (½ stick) butter, softened
1 package (8 ounces) cream cheese, softened
4 cups powdered sugar
1 teaspoon vanilla
1 to 2 tablespoons milk

Beat butter and cream cheese in medium bowl with electric mixer at medium speed until creamy. Gradually beat in powdered sugar and vanilla. Beat until smooth. Add enough milk to make frosting easy to spread.   *Makes 2½ cups frosting*

Oktoberfest

Potato, Beer and Cheese Gratin

1 bottle (12 ounces) pale ale
2 sprigs fresh thyme
1 bay leaf
½ cup heavy cream
1 tablespoon all-purpose flour
2 cloves garlic, pressed or finely minced
2 pounds (about 3 large) potatoes, scrubbed and sliced
1 teaspoon salt
1 teaspoon black pepper
2 cups (8 ounces) shredded Gruyère or Emmenthaler cheese
2 tablespoons chopped chives (optional)

1. Bring pale ale, thyme and bay leaf to a boil in medium saucepan. Reduce heat slightly and stir frequently to eliminate carbonation. Cook 5 minutes or until liquid reduces to about ¾ cup. Remove thyme and bay leaf. Let cool.

2. Combine cream, flour and garlic in small bowl; mix well. Stir into cooled beer mixture.

3. Preheat oven to 375°F. Butter 13×9-inch baking dish. Arrange half of potato slices in bottom of prepared dish, overlapping slightly. Sprinkle with half of salt and pepper. Pour half of cream-beer mixture over potatoes. Sprinkle with half of cheese. Repeat layers.

4. Cover gratin with foil; bake 30 minutes. *Reduce oven temperature to 350°F.* Uncover; bake 30 minutes or until potatoes are tender when poked with knife and top is golden brown. Let stand 10 minutes. Garnish with chives. *Makes 8 servings*

Variation: Add 1 teaspoon of minced jalapeño pepper to the gratin for extra spice and to balance the taste of the beer. Add the jalapeños with the cheese in Step 3.

Wiener Schnitzel

½ cup all-purpose flour
½ teaspoon salt
¼ teaspoon black pepper
2 eggs, beaten
¾ cup dried seasoned bread crumbs
4 slices veal scallopini (about 4 ounces each)
2 tablespoons butter
1 tablespoon olive oil
1 cup brown ale
2 tablespoons capers, drained
4 lemon wedges (optional)

1. Combine flour, salt and pepper in shallow dish; mix well. Place eggs and bread crumbs in 2 shallow dishes. Pat veal scallopini dry. Coat each slice in flour mixture; dip into eggs and then into bread crumbs.

2. Heat butter and oil in large skillet over medium-high heat. Add veal in batches; cook 3 to 4 minutes or until cooked through, turning once. Remove from pan and keep warm.

3. Add ale to pan; bring to a boil, scraping up browned bits from bottom of pan. Cook until mixture is slightly thickened; add capers. Spoon sauce over veal. Garnish with lemon wedges.

Makes 4 servings

TIP: Scallopini is the Italian term for a scallop of meat, which is a thin, boneless piece of meat in an oval shape. Scallops/scallopini are usually breaded and fried, as in this classic recipe. Veal scallopini should be cut across the meat grain for tenderness. When buying scallopini, look at the texture of the meat. The surface should look fairly smooth, not stringy or striated.

Beer and Cheese Soup

2 to 3 slices pumpernickel or rye bread
1 can (about 14 ounces) chicken broth
1 cup beer
¼ cup finely chopped onion
2 cloves garlic, minced
¾ teaspoon dried thyme
1½ cups (6 ounces) shredded American cheese
1½ cups (6 ounces) shredded sharp Cheddar cheese
1 cup milk
½ teaspoon paprika

SLOW COOKER DIRECTIONS

1. Preheat oven to 425°F. Slice bread into ½-inch cubes; place on baking sheet. Bake 10 to 12 minutes or until crisp, stirring once; set aside.

2. Combine broth, beer, onion, garlic and thyme in slow cooker. Cover; cook on LOW 4 hours.

3. *Turn slow cooker to HIGH.* Stir in cheeses, milk and paprika. Cover; cook 45 minutes to 1 hour or until soup is hot and cheeses are melted. Stir soup well to blend cheeses. Ladle soup into bowls; top with croutons. *Makes 4 servings*

Beer and Cheese Soup

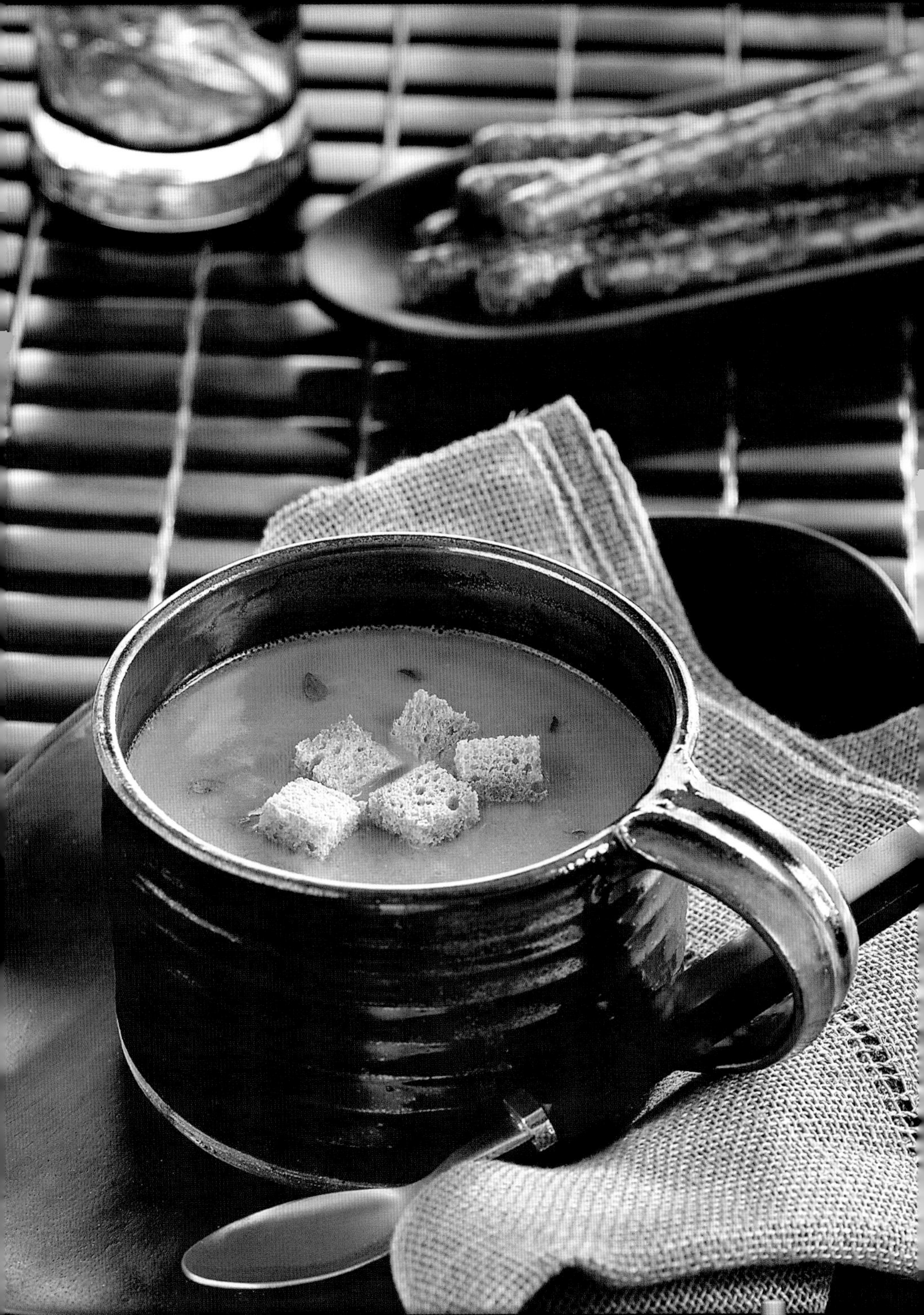

Ale'd Pork and Sauerkraut

1 jar (32 ounces) sauerkraut, undrained
1½ tablespoons sugar
1 can (12 ounces) ale or dark beer
3½ pounds boneless pork shoulder or pork butt roast
½ teaspoon salt
½ teaspoon paprika
¼ teaspoon garlic powder
¼ teaspoon black pepper

SLOW COOKER DIRECTIONS

1. Place sauerkraut in 5-quart slow cooker. Sprinkle with sugar; add ale. Place pork, fat side up, on top of sauerkraut mixture; sprinkle evenly with salt, paprika, garlic powder and black pepper.

2. Cover; cook on HIGH 6 hours.

3. Remove pork to serving platter. Remove sauerkraut with slotted spoon; arrange around pork. Spoon ½ to ¾ cup cooking liquid over sauerkraut.

Makes 6 to 8 servings

TIP: Sauerkraut is German for sour cabbage. Although sauerkraut is a famous German dish, the truth is that most countries have a version of fermented cabbage. In fact, there is some historical evidence that the Chinese had a version of pickled cabbage before the Europeans. If you live near a German or Polish community, try visiting an ethnic store and sampling sauerkraut fresh from the barrel or delicatessen.

Braised Lamb Shanks with Jarlsberg

LAMB

- 4 lamb shanks (about 1 pound each)
- 2 tablespoons extra virgin olive oil
- 1 chopped onion
- 2 cloves garlic, minced
- 1½ cups beer
- 1½ cups beef broth

COATING

- 1 cup (4 ounces) shredded JARLSBERG cheese
- 1 cup flavored bread crumbs
- 1 teaspoon crumbled dried rosemary
- Freshly ground black pepper, to taste
- ⅔ cup cooking liquid from lamb shanks

In large, heavy skillet, brown 4 shanks in olive oil. Add onion and garlic. Cook until golden. Add beer and beef broth; cover; simmer 1½ hours or until fork tender. Remove to platter. To reduce cooking liquid, cook over high heat 5 minutes. Strain, defat and set aside.

Preheat oven to 325°F. Combine cheese with bread crumbs, rosemary, pepper and cooking liquid. Divide mixture into 4 parts. Pat firmly on meaty tops and sides of lamb shanks to "blanket." Place shanks on rack in baking pan. Bake 15 to 20 minutes or until coating is firm and nearly crisp. Serve with white beans, salad and crusty bread. Serve remaining pan juices in gravy boat. *Makes 4 servings*

Brats in Beer

1½ pounds bratwurst (about 5 or 6 links)
  1 bottle (12 ounces) amber ale
  1 medium onion, thinly sliced
  2 tablespoons packed brown sugar
  2 tablespoons red wine vinegar or cider vinegar
    Spicy brown mustard
    Cocktail rye bread

SLOW COOKER DIRECTIONS

1. Combine bratwurst, ale, onion, brown sugar and vinegar in slow cooker. Cover; cook on LOW 4 to 5 hours.

2. Remove bratwurst and onion slices from slow cooker. Cut bratwurst into ½-inch-thick slices. For mini open-faced sandwiches, spread mustard on bread. Top with bratwurst slices and onion. *Makes 30 to 36 appetizers*

Prep Time: 5 minutes • **Cook Time:** 4 to 5 hours

TIP: Slow cookers are great to have around at party time. Set on low, a slow cooker will keep your brats, chili, soup or dip hot and ready to enjoy for hours. Just remember to keep the cooker covered since it looses heat quickly.

Wisconsin Edam and Beer Spread

4 cups shredded Wisconsin Edam cheese*
¾ cup butter, cubed and softened
2 tablespoons snipped fresh chives
2 teaspoons Dijon mustard
½ cup amber or dark beer, at room temperature
  Cocktail rye or pumpernickel bread slices

*Wisconsin Gouda can be substituted for Edam.

Place shredded cheese, butter, chives and mustard in large bowl; mix with spoon until blended. Stir in beer until blended. Chill until serving time. Serve as spread with cocktail bread.   *Makes 4 cups spread*

Variation: Cut one fifth from top of a 2-pound Wisconsin Edam cheese ball to create flat surface. With butter curler or melon baller, remove cheese from center of ball, leaving ½-inch-thick shell. Shred enough of cheese removed from ball and top to measure 4 cups. Reserve any remaining cheese for another use. Follow directions given above to make spread. Spoon spread into hollowed-out cheese ball; reserve remaining spread for refills. Chill until serving time.

Favorite recipe from **Wisconsin Milk Marketing Board**

Ham with Dark Beer Gravy

1 fully cooked bone-in ham half (6 pounds)
1 tablespoon Dijon mustard
2 cans (6 ounces each) pineapple juice
1 bottle (12 ounces) porter
    Dark Beer Gravy (recipe follows)

1. Line large roasting pan with foil.

2. Remove skin and excess fat from ham. Score ham in diamond pattern.

3. Place ham in prepared roasting pan. Spread mustard over ham. Pour pineapple juice and porter over ham. Cover and chill 8 hours.

4. Preheat oven to 350°F. Bake ham 1½ hours or until meat thermometer registers 140°F, basting every 30 minutes. Cover and let stand 15 minutes before slicing. Serve with Dark Beer Gravy. *Makes 16 to 18 servings*

Dark Beer Gravy

2 tablespoons butter
2 tablespoons all-purpose flour
1 cup broth from roasting pan
¼ cup porter
¼ teaspoon salt
⅛ teaspoon black pepper

Melt butter in saucepan over medium heat. Whisk in flour and cook 1 to 2 minutes. Combine broth from roasting pan and porter in small bowl and slowly add to flour mixture. Cook, whisking constantly, until mixture is thickened and bubbly. Add salt and pepper. *Makes 1¼ cups gravy*

Ham with Dark Beer Gravy

Pilsner Parmesan Potatoes

4 pounds Yukon Gold potatoes, peeled and thinly sliced
1 cup minced sweet onion
12 ounces pilsner
1 cup grated Parmesan cheese
½ cup whipping cream
1 tablespoon flour
1 teaspoon paprika
Salt and black pepper

1. Preheat oven to 350°F. Butter 13×9-inch baking dish. Place potato slices in dish. Sprinkle with minced onion.

2. Combine pilsner, Parmesan cheese, cream, flour, paprika, salt and pepper in medium bowl. Pour over potato mixture; stir gently to coat potato slices evenly.

3. Cover baking dish with foil; bake 30 minutes. Remove foil; bake 15 to 20 minutes or until potatoes are golden brown and bubbly. Let stand 15 minutes before serving.

Makes 4 to 6 servings

TIP: Pilsner is a pale lager. It was first brewed in the 19th century in Pilsen, Bohemia. German pilsners tend toward bitter notes compared to American beers. All pilsners are light to golden in color and carry the distinct flavor of hops.

Bratwurst Sandwiches

4 fresh bratwurst (about 1 pound)
1 bottle or can (12 ounces) beer
1 medium onion, sliced
1 small red bell pepper, cut into thin strips
1 small green bell pepper, cut into thin strips
1 tablespoon olive oil
¾ teaspoon salt
½ teaspoon black pepper
4 hoagie or submarine sandwich rolls, split
  Spicy brown or Dijon mustard
  Hot sport peppers (optional)

1. Combine bratwurst and beer in medium saucepan; bring to a boil over high heat. Reduce heat; simmer, uncovered, 20 to 25 minutes or until bratwurst are no longer pink in center, turning occasionally. Cool in liquid. Drain bratwurst; wrap in foil or food storage bag. Refrigerate up to 24 hours.*

2. Combine onion and bell peppers on large sheet of heavy-duty foil. Drizzle with oil and season with salt and pepper. Place another sheet of foil over vegetables; fold up all edges of foil, forming packet. Refrigerate up to 24 hours.*

3. Prepare grill for direct cooking. Place foil packet on grid over medium heat. Cook 5 minutes. Place bratwurst on grid; turn vegetable packet over. Continue grilling 10 minutes or until bratwurst are heated through and vegetables are tender, turning bratwurst once.

4. Place rolls, split sides down, on grid to toast lightly during last 1 to 2 minutes of grilling. Serve bratwurst in rolls topped with vegetables. Serve with mustard and hot peppers, if desired. *Makes 4 servings*

*If tailgating, wrap and refrigerate to transport foods safely to tailgating site. For immediate backyard grilling, wrapping is unnecessary. Cook as directed.

Milwaukee Pork Stew

2 pounds boneless pork shoulder or sirloin, cut into $\frac{1}{2}$-inch cubes
$\frac{1}{3}$ cup all-purpose flour
1 $\frac{1}{2}$ teaspoons salt
$\frac{1}{4}$ teaspoon black pepper
2 tablespoons vegetable oil
4 large onions, sliced $\frac{1}{2}$ inch thick
1 clove garlic, minced
1 can (14$\frac{1}{2}$ ounces) chicken broth
1 can (12 ounces) beer
$\frac{1}{4}$ cup chopped fresh parsley
2 tablespoons red wine vinegar
1 tablespoon packed brown sugar
1 teaspoon caraway seeds
1 bay leaf

Coat pork with combined flour, salt and pepper. Heat oil in Dutch oven; brown meat over medium-high heat. Add onions and garlic. Cook and stir 5 minutes. Pour off drippings. Stir in remaining ingredients. Bring to a boil. Cover; cook over medium-low heat 1 to 1$\frac{1}{4}$ hours or until meat is very tender. Stir occasionally.   *Makes 8 servings*

Preparation Time: 10 minutes • **Cooking Time:** 90 minutes

Favorite recipe from **National Pork Board**

Acknowledgments

The publisher would like to thank the companies and organizations listed below for the use of their recipes in this publication.

Cabot® Creamery Cooperative

Cream of Wheat® Cereal

Jennie-O Turkey Store, LLC

National Honey Board

National Pork Board

Norseland, Inc.

Reckitt Benckiser Inc.

Unilever

Wisconsin Milk Marketing Board

METRIC CONVERSION CHART

VOLUME MEASUREMENTS (dry)

$^{1}/_{8}$ teaspoon = 0.5 mL
$^{1}/_{4}$ teaspoon = 1 mL
$^{1}/_{2}$ teaspoon = 2 mL
$^{3}/_{4}$ teaspoon = 4 mL
1 teaspoon = 5 mL
1 tablespoon = 15 mL
2 tablespoons = 30 mL
$^{1}/_{4}$ cup = 60 mL
$^{1}/_{3}$ cup = 75 mL
$^{1}/_{2}$ cup = 125 mL
$^{2}/_{3}$ cup = 150 mL
$^{3}/_{4}$ cup = 175 mL
1 cup = 250 mL
2 cups = 1 pint = 500 mL
3 cups = 750 mL
4 cups = 1 quart = 1 L

VOLUME MEASUREMENTS (fluid)

1 fluid ounce (2 tablespoons) = 30 mL
4 fluid ounces ($^{1}/_{2}$ cup) = 125 mL
8 fluid ounces (1 cup) = 250 mL
12 fluid ounces (1$^{1}/_{2}$ cups) = 375 mL
16 fluid ounces (2 cups) = 500 mL

WEIGHTS (mass)

$^{1}/_{2}$ ounce = 15 g
1 ounce = 30 g
3 ounces = 90 g
4 ounces = 120 g
8 ounces = 225 g
10 ounces = 285 g
12 ounces – 360 g
16 ounces = 1 pound = 450 g

DIMENSIONS

$^{1}/_{16}$ inch = 2 mm
$^{1}/_{8}$ inch = 3 mm
$^{1}/_{4}$ inch = 6 mm
$^{1}/_{2}$ inch = 1.5 cm
$^{3}/_{4}$ inch = 2 cm
1 inch = 2.5 cm

OVEN TEMPERATURES

250°F = 120°C
275°F = 140°C
300°F = 150°C
325°F = 160°C
350°F = 180°C
375°F = 190°C
400°F = 200°C
425°F = 220°C
450°F = 230°C

BAKING PAN SIZES

Utensil	Size in Inches/Quarts	Metric Volume	Size in Centimeters
Baking or Cake Pan (square or rectangular)	8×8×2	2 L	20×20×5
	9×9×2	2.5 L	23×23×5
	12×8×2	3 L	30×20×5
	13×9×2	3.5 L	33×23×5
Loaf Pan	8×4×3	1.5 L	20×10×7
	9×5×3	2 L	23×13×7
Round Layer Cake Pan	8×1½	1.2 L	20×4
	9×1½	1.5 L	23×4
Pie Plate	8×1¼	750 mL	20×3
	9×1¼	1 L	23×3
Baking Dish or Casserole	1 quart	1 L	—
	1½ quart	1.5 L	—
	2 quart	2 L	—